Historical Association of Ireland
Life and Times Series, No. 2

Sir Edward Carson

ALVIN JACKSON

Published for the
HISTORICAL ASSOCIATION OF IRELAND
~~By Dundalgan Press Ltd~~

First published 1993
ISBN 0-85221-122-8

To
Brian Harrison

Cover design: Jarlath Hayes
Historical Association of Ireland, Dublin
Printed by Dundalgan Pr̶e̶s̶s̶ ̶D̶

FOREWORD

This series of short biographical studies published by the Historical Association of Ireland is designed to place the lives of leading historical figures against the background of new research on the problems and conditions of their times. These studies should be particularly helpful to students preparing for Leaving Certificate, G.C.E. Advanced Level and undergraduate history examinations, while at the same time appealing to the general public.

CIARAN BRADY
EUGENE J. DOYLE
Historical Association of Ireland

PREFACE

I am grateful to Keith Jeffery, University of Ulster, and to Michael Laffan, University College, Dublin, for their acute comments on an earlier version of this text. I am also grateful to Robert Bell of the Linen Hall Library, Belfast, for help with source materials, and to Anthony Malcomson, Deputy Keeper of the Public Record Office of Northern Ireland, for permission to use the papers in his care. Lord Craigavon, Lord Londonderry and the families of the late H. M. Hyde and the late Sir Wilfrid Spender granted me access to materials on deposit in P.R.O.N.I.

ALVIN JACKSON
Department of Modern History
Queen's University of Belfast

CONTENTS

CHRONOLOGY OF CARSON'S LIFE AND TIMES

1854 9 Feb.: Carson born at 4 Harcourt Street, Dublin. 14 Sept.: British and French landings on the Crimea.

1858 17 Mar.: creation of Irish Republican Brotherhood.

1871 28 Jan.: armistice signed between France and Prussia. Oct.: Carson enters Trinity College, Dublin.

1877 April: Carson sits his bar finals, King's Inns.

1879 20 April: land agitation launched in Mayo. 21 Oct.: creation of the Irish National Land League. 19 Dec: Carson marries Annette Kirwan at Monkstown parish church, Dublin.

1881 Jan.: death of his father. 7 April: introduction of Land Law (Ireland) Bill in House of Commons.

1885 1 May: creation of the Irish Loyal and Patriotic Union in Dublin. Nov.–Dec.: Carson campaigns on behalf of Liberal Unionist cause in Dublin. 17 Dec.: announcement of Gladstone's conversion to Home Rule.

1886 8 April: introduction of Home Rule Bill into House of Commons. 8 June: defeat of Home Rule Bill. June–Sept.: intermittent rioting in Belfast. July: Carson campaigns on behalf of Liberal Unionist cause. 23 Oct.: publication of the Plan of Campaign in *United Ireland.*

1887 7 Mar.: Arthur Balfour appointed Chief Secretary for Ireland. 19 July : Criminal Law and Procedure Act—Carson appointed crown prosecutor. 9 Sept.: 'Mitchelstown Massacre'—trials of William O'Brien and John Mandeville.

1889 24 June: Carson appointed Q.C. 24 Dec.: beginning of O'Shea divorce proceedings.

1890 1–6 Dec.: Committee Room Fifteen Debate—split in the Irish Parliamentary Party after withdrawal of Justin McCarthy.

1891 6 Oct.: death of Parnell.

1892 17 June: Ulster Convention, Belfast. 1 July: Carson appointed Solicitor General for Ireland. 8 July: elected Liberal Unionist M.P. for the University of Dublin.

1893 2 Feb.: Carson's maiden speech in Commons. 13 Feb.: introduction of the second Home Rule Bill.

1895 3 April: opening of Oscar Wilde's prosecution of Marquis of Queensberry.

1896 Feb.: appointed to the Irish Privy Council. 14 Aug.: Land Law (Ireland) Act passed (despite Carson's bitter opposition).

1898 13 Jan.: creation of United Irish League. 12 Aug.: Local Government (Ireland) Act passed.

1899 11 Oct.: outbreak of war in South Africa.

1900 May: appointed Solicitor General for England.

1903 25 Mar.: introduction of Wyndham's land purchase bill (Carson unsympathetic).

1905 3 Mar.: first public meeting, Ulster Unionist Council. Dec.: Privy Counsellor for England. 4 Dec.: resignation of Conservative government.

1907 5 Sept.: amalgamation of National Council and Sinn Féin League as Sinn Féin.

1910 Jan.–Feb.: general election in United Kingdom (Irish Nationalists hold balance in House of Commons). 21 Feb.: Carson accepts leadership of the Irish Unionist Parliamentary Party. July: Archer-Shee trial. Dec.: general election in United Kingdom (Irish Nationalists hold balance).

1911 23 Jan.: formation of Ulster Women's Unionist Council. 18 Aug.: Parliament Act on statute book. 23 Sept.: Craigavon demonstration. 8 Nov.: Balfour resigns Conservative leadership—Carson refuses to contest the succession.

1912 11 April: introduction of the third Home Rule Bill. 11 June: Agar-Robartes amendment. 28 Sept.: Covenant Day, Ulster.

1913 1 Jan.: Carson introduces nine-county exclusion amendment to the Home Rule Bill. 31 Jan.: U.V.F. formally inaugurated. 6 April: death of Annette Carson. 26 Aug.: beginning of Dublin tram strike and lock-out. 24 Sept.: formation of the Ulster Provisional Government. 25 Nov.: formation of the Irish Volunteers. 4 Dec.: prohibition of weapons imports into Ireland.

1914 20 Mar.: Curragh 'incident'. 24–5 April: Larne gun-running. 12 May: announcement of amending bill to the Home Rule measure. 28 June: assassination of Franz Ferdinand at Sarajevo. 21–4 July: Buckingham Palace Conference. 23 July: Austro-Hungarian ultimatum to Serbia. 26 July: Howth gun-running. 4 Aug.: war between United Kingdom and Germany. 15 Sept.: suspension of the Home Rule Act.

1915 25 May: Carson appointed Attorney General in Asquith coalition ministry.

1916 24–9 April: Easter Rising, Dublin. 23 May–24 July: Lloyd George negotiations on Irish government. 12 June: Ulster Unionist Council accepts Carson's defence of Lloyd George scheme. 1 July: opening of Battle of the Somme. Nov.–Dec.: Carson helps to oust Asquith. 7 Dec.: appointed First Lord of the Admiralty.

1917 8–15 Mar.: 'February Revolution' in Russia. 21 May: Irish Convention scheme published. 7 July: Carson moved from the

Admiralty to membership of the war cabinet. 10 July: election of de Valera for East Clare. 25–6 Oct.: Sinn Féin *ard-fheis*. 6–7 Nov. 1917: 'October Revolution' in Russia.

1918 22 Jan.: Carson resigns from war cabinet. 6 Mar.: death of John Redmond. April–May: anti-conscription protest. 11 Nov.: armistice between Germany and the Allied powers. 14–28 Dec.: general election (73 Sinn Féin, 6 I.P.P., 26 Unionists returned): Carson elected for Duncairn division (Belfast).

1919 21 Jan.: Soloheadbeg ambush; first meeting of Dáil Éireann. 28 June: signing of the Treaty of Versailles. 7 Oct.: cabinet committee formed to consider Irish government.

1920 25 Feb.: introduction of Government of Ireland Bill (Carson lukewarm). 20 Mar.: Ulster Unionist Council accepts Government of Ireland Bill.

1921 4 Feb.: Carson resigns as leader of Ulster Unionism. 21 May: Carson accepts judicial office as Lord of Appeal (Lord Carson of Duncairn). 9 July: truce between crown forces and I.R.A. 6 Dec.: Anglo-Irish Treaty signed in London. 14 Dec.: Carson bitterly condemns Treaty in House of Lords.

1922 28 Oct.: Mussolini's march on Rome.

1929 29 Oct.: collapse of share prices on Wall Street. 1 Nov.: Carson retires from the Court of Appeal.

1932 Publication of Edward Marjoribanks's *Life of Lord Carson.*

1933 30 Jan.: Hitler appointed German Chancellor. 8 July: unveiling of Carson's statue at Stormont, Belfast.

1934 Publication of Ian Colvin's second volume of the *Life of Lord Carson*

1935 2 Oct.: Italian invasion of Abyssinia. 22 Oct.: Carson dies at Cleve Court, Ramsgate. 26 Oct.: state funeral, St Anne's Cathedral, Belfast.

1936 Publication of Colvin's third volume of the *Life of Lord Carson.*

INTRODUCTION

The fiction of the stage comes closer to reality than the 'facts' of historiography. And perhaps this is appropriate, for undoubtedly the histrionic element in Sir Edward Carson's personality ran deep. Terence Rattigan's play 'The Winslow Boy', inspired by one of Carson's greatest legal triumphs, charts the fluid emotions of the lawyer as he melts from hectoring aggression to paternal sentimentality; the play conveys something of the neurotic motor force behind Carson's superficial confidence and poise—something of the foppishness behind his rather puritanical exterior.[1] Here is the authentic Carson, as betrayed in his most private moments, and in his most intimate correspondence: this is the ambiguous and vulnerable Carson observed by his wife, by women friends like Theresa Londonderry and by the men closest to him (such as Tommy Comyn-Platt). It is not always the Carson of the polemicists, or, indeed, the textbooks. Here both Unionist and Nationalist observers conspire to present a lantern-jawed Uebermensch to their readers, whether as the Bismarckian creator of Northern Ireland or the Hitlerian demagogue of the 1912–14 era.[2]

These myths are important both as a revelation of what Irish people want to believe about Carson, and as a testimony to the efficiency of the Ulster Unionist propagandists who manufactured Carson's public image: these myths have an independent historical force and function. But they do not add up to a complete portrayal of Carson, nor do they help in unravelling the complexities and apparent contradictions within his personality and actions. Carson, the arch-conservative of 1921, was—as the Northern Nationalist, Joe Devlin, always remembered—the devout liberal of 1881; Carson, the landlord apologist of the 1890s, was the hero of demotic urban Unionism between 1910 and 1921; Carson, the quintessential lawyer, was (apparently) the most brazen subverter of legal procedure in 1913–14; Carson, a thoroughgoing Irish Unionist, came to be revered (or traduced) as the master-builder of the partition settlement. He was the

4

true-blue Tory who changed political shading with the facility of a chameleon; he was the embodiment both of a brute machismo and a perpetually alert sensitivity.

This little book is not, by definition, a full-scale biography (such as those written by Edward Marjoribanks and Ian Colvin or by H. M. Hyde). Neither is it a reduced, or miniature, 'life' (such as those by J. V. Bates or A. T. Q. Stewart).[3] It is certainly hoped that as full a portrait of Carson will be offered as is compatible with the constraints both of space and of the surviving evidence. However, this portrait will be constructed, not through a rigidly chronological progression, but by examining the several principles which comprised Carson's political creed: the law, the land, Unionism, ministerial service. This is therefore a thematic biography, although the themes have been organised so as to preserve a sense of chronological development. In addition, the book opens with a discussion of Carson's personality, and closes with a survey of his legal and political achievements.

1

PERSONALITY

'A pious imputation of consistency [is] the besetting fault of most political biography,' R. F. Foster has written.[1] The published details of Carson's life suggest, indeed, a confident evolution from his birth in middle-class Dublin, in 1854, through an obstreperous boyhood and playfully aggressive adolescence, to the mature and militant politician of the Edwardian era. Carson, the unyielding advocate of Ulster Unionism in 1912, is scarcely to be distinguished from the pugnacious little boy of the 1860s or the brash undergraduate at Trinity College, Dublin, in the 1870s. At school at Arlington House, Queen's County, he was—his biographers affirm—a dedicated opponent of bullying; and, in a premonition of his later, political career, it is recorded that he bravely took on those older, bigger and more brutal than himself. At Trinity (where he distinguished himself neither as an examinee nor on the sports fields), he boldly confronted the college authorities, just as in later life he faced down the Liberal government of H. H. Asquith.[2]

Allusions such as these dominate the published accounts of Carson's early life, and they serve to emphasise his undoubted truculence and his unquestionable moral courage: they foreshadow the qualities of political leadership by which he is best remembered. Carson was, indeed, often truculent both as a boy and as a man, taking on opponents apparently more powerful than himself. Yet this 'pious imputation of consistency' in the biographical record obscures as much as it illuminates, for Carson was much more than the 'hard man' perceived by his militant admirers. Carson in retirement was anxious about his reputation and informed these accounts both of schoolboy derring-do and of his juvenile passion for justice. But this very concern for image and reputation should alert us to the existence of a rather more vulnerable figure within the intricate shell of Victorian manliness.[3]

Theresa, Marchioness of Londonderry, was one of Carson's closest friends, and she was among the very few with whom he regularly corresponded.[4] She saw in him not simply a firm and charismatic politician, but a depressive, anguished by periods of exhaustion and doubt, and racked in later life by a nagging fear of physical and mental collapse. She saw, through his letters, a man of uncertain temperament who, though renowned for his political temerity, could be—in some matters—irritatingly timid. Though an admirer, Theresa Londonderry was perpetually infuriated by Carson's diffidence when offered ministerial promotion. Though an admirer, she was often angered by Carson's lugubriousness and lack of vigour. She also felt (as some others did) that his second marriage to Ruby Frewen, 'a woman thirty years younger than himself, and not too clever a one at that', had been a disastrous distraction from public affairs.[5]

Carson's vulnerable health and his profound sense of mortality help to explain his swings between aggressive self-assertion and utter collapse. As a child he was diagnosed as having a weak heart, although this did not prevent him becoming embroiled in schoolboy fights or in playing hurling as a student at Trinity (this last is an interesting affirmation of Carson's enthusiastic Irishness). As a young man he contracted typhoid and came close to death. In his mid-twenties he was also plagued by gallstones, then regarded as a more dangerous and debilitating complaint than now. He survived these trials, but disease and death were a more than usually stark presence throughout his early life. His father died in 1881, when Carson was twenty-seven. James Shannon, who was the same age as Carson, and who had been a close friend at school, at college and on circuit, died in the same year. Carson's first love, Katie Lambert, also died at around this time: like Shannon, she had not yet reached thirty.[6]

But, to a very great extent, his ill-health, and his anxiety, were self-induced. He worked too hard. He was not a naturally brilliant student: success came only in modest portions, and only then after intense labour.[7] He struggled to master the intricacies of his legal textbooks, and—later—devoted lavish attention to the preparation of his cases. Overwork and professional insecurity made Carson liable to anxieties concerning his health and his prospects, and this led frequently to intense depression.

Throughout the early and mid-1880s he battled to win a reputation in the courtrooms of the Leinster Circuit, earning meanwhile a modest and highly precarious income. In July 1887 a new and more sweeping crimes act—the Criminal Law and Procedure (Ireland) Act—was passed, which indirectly brought Carson greater security, but only at the cost of intense professional strain. At the age of thirty-three he was appointed a crown prosecutor, with the task of assisting the Attorney General for Ireland in enforcing the crimes act. But though he performed his official duties with zeal and efficiency—Parnellites soon dubbed him 'Coercion Carson'—the toll on his precarious health was severe. And, while his growing band of admirers confidently foresaw a brilliant parliamentary and ministerial career for the thrusting young lawyer, Carson soon sought escape from the brutal demands of his advocacy: in 1888 he applied (unsuccessfully) for the relative ease and anonymity of a county court judgeship.[8]

Neither professional nor political success copper-fastened Carson's confidence; success did not promote any more secure faith in his own health or capacity. After 1892, when he entered the House of Commons, Carson enjoyed a remarkable professional and political prominence which is described in the following chapters, and which culminated in 1910, when he was chosen to lead the Irish Unionist Parliamentary Party and the Ulster Unionist movement. Yet this eminence was built on the insecure foundations of a neurotic personality and weak health. Carson's success owed a great deal to his capacity for hard work, but this in turn often meant exhaustion and worry. His domination of the English bar in the later 1890s, and his developing parliamentary stature only served to increase his burdens and the strain on his mind and on his health. Sustained periods of political and professional labour were invariably followed by weeks of physical and nervous prostration.

As he grew older, and richer, so he became more vulnerable to collapse, and withal better able to cope with its consequences. After a particularly difficult parliamentary session or law term Carson would normally retreat either to a German spa town, such as Bad Homburg, or to his own country house at Rottingdean in Kent, or to the home of an aristocratic friend. In later life he would simply take to his bed and write self-pitying letters designed to engage the sympathies of his few close friends. On at least one occasion, in January 1916, Carson's exhaustion and retreat from politics gave rise to rumours that he was suffering from some serious ailment and had (permanently) retired. This and similar challenges invariably spurred him into action and converted his morbid self-pity into an altogether more healthy anger.[9]

Carson's depression seems also to have been rooted in his personal circumstances. His first marriage, to Annette Kirwan, was broken only by her death in April 1913. Annette never fully adjusted to Carson's meteoric rise to professional and political prominence, and in particular she hated their move to London in 1892–3. She felt that she was socially out of her depth, and she resented the extent to which her husband was lionised in the Conservative salons. She felt, with some justification, that she was neglected by Carson. Carson's (entirely platonic) relationships with other women created great difficulties, which came to a head over his intense and rather sentimental correspondence with Theresa Londonderry.[10]

Annette found solace in gambling, an enthusiasm which she passed on to her eldest son, Harry. Harry and his siblings offered little compensating relief or diversion to their father: 'my children are a rum lot,' a misanthropic Carson grumbled in 1913.[11] Harry's improvidence remained a nagging worry, as did the ill-health and romantic susceptibility of his sister, Gladys (Gladys seems to have inherited Carson's nervous vulnerability, for in February 1918 she fell victim to 'acute hysteria').[12] Strained relations with his wife and the problems created by his children unquestionably helped to nudge Carson into the black depressions which pursued him to the grave.

Despite his ill-health both as a boy and as a man, and despite the stress of his work and the anxieties created by his family, Carson outlived many of his contemporaries (Bonar Law, Asquith) and many prominent politicians considerably younger than himself (F. E. Smith, George Wyndham): he died, in his bed, at the age of eighty-one. He was ultimately a victim of leukaemia, rather than of his nerves or a 'tired' heart or the other ailments of which he habitually complained. Was he, then, merely a worka-holic who exaggerated the significance of perfectly common ailments and perfectly ordinary swings of mood? One of his earliest and most sympathetic biographers, Ian Colvin, described Carson as a hypochondriac while Carson was still alive and might presumably have taken offence.[13] Yet perhaps Carson was not unhappy with this description, for his real malady was possibly rather more serious than Colvin had suggested. Carson was diagnosed by his doctors as a neurasthenic. This was an umbrella term which covered a variety of physical and nervous conditions. Colvin later argued (in 1936) that Carson's 'neurasthenia' sprang from a 'lifelong internal pain'; and Colvin maintained that, while the exact source of this pain eluded the doctors, its nagging and debilitating presence weakened Carson and intensified his morbid concern for his health.[14] But neurasthenia was also used in the Great War as a diagnostic label for shell-shock and for cases involving a profound mental collapse.

Carson's malady was more than a sciatic pain, and much less serious than the condition of the 'neurasthenic' casualties of the First World War. He had high blood pressure; he was probably a clinical depressive. Yet, while his mental and physical health never permanently broke down, this discussion has much more than a narrowly personal interest. For health was an obsession, and health-related anxieties had a profound impact upon Carson's career. His periodic exhaustion and loss of confidence and depression help to illuminate some of the apparent inconsistencies within the received image of the man, his personality and his actions. His preferred public face—the vigorous, unyielding diehard—was, to some extent, a debilitating theatrical performance which frequently concealed a politically more pliable, a more vulnerable, and a more sensitive figure: 'there was a quality which he strived to conceal,' Colvin remarked, 'a tenderness of heart'.[15] The image of the unyielding diehard was also in part the shared fabrication of Ulster Unionist publicists and, ironically, Irish Parliamentary Party critics.[16] Ulster Unionists like James Craig promoted Carson as an immovably reliable leader; Irish Nationalists like John Redmond represented Carson as an immovable extremist whose unthinking truculence threatened the integrity of Ireland. These images, though important, were not the totality of Carson's personality and politics. But it suited Carson's ends to play the invulnerable commander—even if the theatrical effort induced anxiety and depression and led to a bed-ridden retreat.

On 9 September 1887 O'Brien and John Mandeville, a gentleman farmer and M.P. from Clonkilla, Mitchelstown, County Cork, were summoned to appear before a Resident Magistrate at Mitchelstown to answer a charge of incitement. Rather than meekly submitting to the authority of the crown, the two men decided to milk the opportunities for publicity through a show of defiance. They held a protest demonstration and roused the local farmers on behalf of the Plan of Campaign. A riot ensued. The ill-prepared and weakly led police panicked and opened fire. Three men were killed, the victims of what became known as the 'Mitchelstown Massacre'. Two weeks later Carson successfully prosecuted O'Brien for incitement; in October 1887 Carson represented the crown during the appeal hearing. O'Brien was jailed for three months and maintained his defiance by refusing to submit to the prison regime; incarcerated, he acquired both a pair of Blarney tweed breeches and a national celebrity. His colleague, John Mandeville, more vulnerable than O'Brien, later died as a result of his privations in Tullamore jail.

Carson had been at Mitchelstown on 9 September, the day of the killings; Carson had been the most public, if not the chief, agent of the Castle administration in its pursuit of O'Brien. For Carson, and for his patrons, Mitchelstown was a loyalist rite of passage. The prosecution of O'Brien demanded no particular technical finesse, but it required both moral and physical courage; the prosecution was the first and the most public case taken by the Castle under the terms of the draconian crimes act. Carson's bravura performance during the trial, and the successful conviction of O'Brien, had therefore a very wide resonance. This and later bold prosecutions won for Carson the admiration of Arthur Balfour and of loyalist Ireland. Conservative northerners, who had been suspicious of the liberal and tenant-right enthusiasms of the young lawyer, now saw Carson as a stalwart friend to law and order and as a champion of the Union. Nationalists, on the other hand, were confused and dismayed by what they described as Carson's treachery and venality: 'you think', he was told by O'Brien's defence counsel, Timothy Harrington, 'that by this display you will get some position from the Tory government for whom you are doing this job'.[5]

Carson emerged from Mitchelstown as simultaneously a hero
of the Union and a bloody coercionist: his modern reputation in
Ireland had already been fixed, therefore, by the autumn of 1887.
Later prosecutions only served to secure his place in the
Nationalist demonology, and to confirm his indispensability to
Dublin Castle. Harrington had utterly misinterpreted and
traduced Carson's principles, but he was unquestionably right
about the rewards of serving the Castle administration. In 1889
Carson became, at the age of thirty-five, the youngest Q.C. in
Ireland; on 1 July 1892, during the last days of the Salisbury
government, he was installed as Solicitor General for Ireland; and
on 8 July he was returned (after a controversial intervention on
his behalf by Balfour) as junior member of parliament for Dublin
University.[6] Balfour claimed that he had 'made' Carson, and—
though they were separated in age by only six years—Carson
never lost a sense of filial obligation to his old Chief Secretary.[7]

The Irish bar of the 1880s was a testing and brutal school for an
ambitious young lawyer. But the diversity of the experience which
Carson gained—the diversity of legal and pyschological insight—
offered sure foundations for the rest of his career. Success in
Ireland, the loyal patronage of Balfour, and a swiftly won parliamentary celebrity (his maiden speech created immense excite-
ment)—all these encouraged Carson to wind down his Irish
practice and to venture into the more lucrative and challenging
English bar. He took this decision in January 1893, and was called
at the Middle Temple, in London, in April of that year. It was a
bold, some thought a foolhardy move, yet it was entirely typical of
the calculated rashness which Carson displayed throughout his
life.[8] Carson loved advocacy, and—short of promotion to the
bench—he had achieved everything which the Irish legal system
had to offer. In the 1890s, an era when court cases were reported in
detail, and when leading barristers such as Sir Edward Clarke and
Sir Charles Russell were venerated as secular saints, the English
courts were an obvious focus of ambition. Lawyers increasingly
dominated parliamentary politics, and the fees of the most
prominent rivalled the annual rental income of some of Britain's
wealthier landed magnates. The rewards of success were glorious,
and yet—for Carson—the risk was calculated. He had earned
enough in Ireland to provide a financial reserve if all went awry; he

had, as has been observed, a parliamentary base and first-class political patronage as professional collateral. There was the encouraging evidence of those several Irish barristers (such as Russell) who had made good. And, if all went wrong, the opportunity remained of returning to Ireland to reconstruct his reputation. Carson's inexorable progress at the English bar has been charted many times. He was made an English Q.C. in 1895, after only two years of professional practice; in 1900 he was appointed Solicitor General for England, a junior ministerial post, but one reserved for only the ablest parliamentary lawyers. By 1899–1900 he was earning some £20,000 a year in fees, and was allegedly turning away briefs worth in total £30,000.[9] He was perhaps the wealthiest, the most successful, lawyer of these years at the end of the nineteenth century. His professional standing was, before the emergence of younger, hungrier rivals such as Rufus Isaacs or F. E. Smith, ascendant. He excelled in cross-examination, choosing his opening questions with precision; he could be aggressive, but he was not by nature a bully, and in any case such tactics could easily be counter-productive.[10] He invented, instead, a cold impersonal style of prosecution: sharp, remorseless, but detached.[11] He could be quietly and politely insistent. 'No man', Lord Beaverbrook said of Carson, 'possessed a greater or more overwhelming charm of manner'; and this charm was often deployed, and often devastated.[12]

Marjoribanks and Hyde, Carson's first and greatest biographers, were each barristers, and they each offered in their work an intricate dissection of their subject's various legal triumphs.[13] There is no need to replicate their accounts here. But in the long span of Carson's career at the English bar three cases are of inescapable significance: the first Oscar Wilde trial (1895), the Osborne case (1910), and the Marconi case (1913). Each of these victories enhanced Carson's professional and political standing in particular ways; but, though they play a central role in triumphalist accounts of Carson's career, their importance goes beyond what might be immediately obvious.

Victorian courtrooms were unfailing sources of salacious material to a prurient public; and successful lawyers occupied a role not dissimilar to the bishops of the early church, attracting reverence both for their social position and for their work as moral custodians. No case satisfied late Victorian prurience more than the trials of Oscar Wilde; and no case defined Carson's ethics more sharply in the public mind. Carson emerged from what Mr Justice Collins called 'the filth' of the trial as a vigorous prosecutor of vice, and as an unbending proponent of public morality.[14]

In reality Carson never prosecuted Wilde, and indeed actively advised against his prosecution. Carson was instead a reluctant defence counsel in a case of libel brought by Wilde against the Marquis of Queensberry. Queensberry had addressed a card to the playwright, which contained the implication that Wilde had been guilty of homosexual activity (which was punishable under the Criminal Law Amendment Act of 1885): 'To Oscar Wilde, posing Somdomite [sic]'.[15] Wilde, relying perhaps on his social connections, and confident that no evidence could be brought to justify this allegation, decided to prosecute on a charge of criminal libel. Carson agreed to defend Queensberry, but only after considerable soul-searching and anxious discussions with professional intimates and father-figures (such as Lord Halsbury, a former Conservative Lord Chancellor). The defence was successful. Evidence was adduced linking Wilde to a circle of rent-boys and thereby confirming Queensberry's allegation. Wilde's prosecution collapsed, and Queensberry was acquitted.

The salacious nature of the case, the confrontation between a famous dramatist and a famous sportsman, the incidental involvement of other prominent figures, all ensured massive publicity: it was, as Montgomery Hyde observed, 'the most sensational trial of the "nineties"'.[16] Carson's role, and his forensic triumph in cross-examining Wilde, won him a celebrity equivalent only to that which he had left behind in Dublin. The successful defence of Queensberry provided the basis for Carson's flourishing practice in the later 1890s and bolstered his credibility and reputation within the House of Commons: 'what made Carson unmade Wilde,' as Richard Ellmann has drily observed.[17] Through the defence of Queensberry Carson entered into the world of Oscar Wilde, and therefore into the realms of literary controversy and mythology. In films he is the brusque and brutal lawyer who broke Wilde and helped to thrust him to disgrace and to an early grave.[18] In biographies of Wilde, such as the masterpiece by Ellmann, he is scarcely less of a stage villain.

The contemporary reality was, perhaps, more subtle than this. Carson had initially rejected the brief for Queensberry on the grounds of his own acquaintance with Wilde at Trinity and the thinness of the evidence against the playwright. He changed his mind having received the advice of one of the most authoritative lawyers of the day, Halsbury; and he confirmed his decision when the connection between Wilde and the rent-boys became irrefutable. After Queensberry was acquitted, Wilde was arrested and tried on a charge of indecency. Carson refused to take any part in this prosecution, and indeed—after the trial jury had disagreed and had been dismissed—he urged that the case be dropped.[19]

Judged by contemporaries as a moral titan, and by historians as a homophobic puritan, the truth was that Carson, as always, was true to the demands of his profession. He was sensitive to Wilde's plight. There was a story, current until the 1930s, that Carson had encountered Wilde in exile in Paris, had accidentally knocked him down, and proffered only an icy 'I beg your pardon' by way of apology. Had it been true, the story would have neatly illustrated the hostility which allegedly drove Carson. But it was apocryphal: 'if he [Carson] had knocked Wilde over', the eighty-year-old Carson told Ian Colvin, 'he would have said more than that cold "I beg your pardon"; he would have helped him to his feet, and to his hotel'.[20] In private Carson undoubtedly thought that Wilde was a charlatan and a poseur; but he did not pursue any antagonism.[21] Once he had accepted the brief for Queensberry, he thought only of the interests of his client. For he was the consummate barrister.

Thirteen years later, in the autumn of 1908, a young naval cadet was accused of theft, and there began the second of the great cases which decided Carson's professional reputation. George Archer-Shee was a pupil at the Royal Naval College at Osborne, on the Isle of Wight. In October 1908, after a series of thefts, he was expelled: a postal order for five shillings had been stolen from one of the other boys, and an investigation by the college authorities speedily inculpated young George. Here, with the disgrace of a little boy, the affair might well have rested, had it not been for George's step-brother, who was a Conservative M.P., and therefore a colleague of Carson. Martin Archer-Shee brought the case to Carson's attention and won his interest—but it was George himself who convinced the lawyer of his innocence (though only after a lengthy and bruising interrogation). In July 1910, after considerable barracking by his advocate, George's case was brought to the High Court.

During the trial Carson quietly demolished the witnesses for the crown and skilfully harnessed the evident integrity of the Archer-Shee family. The crown case collapsed, and young George emerged as a wounded innocent. He was completely exonerated; the confidence of his family was thoroughly vindicated.[22]

But the importance of the case had been scarcely more marked for the Archer-Shees than for their advocate. Carson regarded the successful defence of George as 'the happiest moment of his life at the bar': the victory was a cause for joyful tears.[23] Apart from pride and sentimentality, there were more tangible rewards of victory. As with the Wilde trial, this was a case which attracted considerable publicity and helped to reformulate the popular image of Carson. His ascendancy at the bar was apparently confirmed, despite the mounting challenge of younger men: the Archer-Shee case was, in fact, the most conspicuous of the many forensic duels fought between Carson and Rufus Isaacs (who acted for the crown). The fame of the case also recast Carson's popular reputation in a rather softer and gentler light: the lawyer basked in the radiance of George Archer-Shee's boyish integrity. Carson had successfully challenged a bullying and insensitive bureaucracy on behalf of a vulnerable child; he had defended a manly little servant of the King-Emperor against a ruthless enemy. It was the stuff of popular Edwardian fiction and of melodrama; indeed, the case eventually found its way onto the stage and the silver screen as Terence Rattigan's 'The Winslow Boy'.[24] For thousands who knew little of the Edwardian bar, or who cared little for Irish Unionism, Carson was instantly recognised and revered as Rattigan's Sir Robert Morton, K.C., an icily urbane lawyer who could yet dissolve into tears and sentimentality. This fictional confection was not far removed from the authentic Carson.

The Archer-Shee case had an importance for Carson's view of Irish policy. It helped simultaneously to convince him of the bureaucratic tyranny of Asquith's government, and to persuade him that this tyranny might be overcome by moral strength and political persistence. He saw an insensitive First Lord of the Admiralty and Attorney General enshroud justice and right with legalistic formulae and pedantry; he saw ministers use the forms of law to commit acts of oppression. These insights undoubtedly helped to determine Carson's strategies as Ulster Unionist leader in 1912–14, when he defied what he saw as a dictatorial government, and sought his own vision of justice beyond the confines of the law.

There was an overlap between the Osborne case and a later highly charged and resonant trial in which Carson was closely involved: the Marconi affair. Many of the personalities engaged in the trial of George Archer-Shee reappeared as the Marconi scandal developed in 1912–13; some of the passion generated by the Archer-Shee trial was transferred across to the Marconi case. But the significance of Marconi radiated far more widely than Archer-Shee; and the political implications of the affair for Carson were more immediate and more profound.[25]

The Marconi scandal was a volatile concoction of ministerial impropriety, indeed corruption, political dishonesty and vindictiveness, and an aggressive antisemitism. This was a compound which ignited party politics and enthralled and enraged a prurient British public; it was a compound which very nearly destroyed Asquith's Liberal ministry. At the root of the affair was the suggestion that four government ministers had been involved in the illegal purchase and sale of Marconi shares: the accused were David Lloyd George (the Chancellor of the Exchequer), the Master of Elibank (the Liberal Chief Whip), Sir Rufus Isaacs (the Attorney General), and Herbert Samuel (the Postmaster General). The Chief Whip resigned from his post and from his parliamentary seat in the summer of 1912 for reasons unconnected with Marconi; the charge against Samuel was clearly the most attenuated element of the case against the ministers. It was therefore on Lloyd George and Isaacs that the weight of public and parliamentary opprobrium came to rest. It was these ministers who were pursued with the greatest ruthlessness in the House of Commons from the autumn of 1912, when the scandal broke, through to the early summer of 1913, when the final Marconi debate took place. The Conservative opposition sensed that Lloyd George and Isaacs were wounded prey, and stalked the ministers with an appropriate ferocity. But Carson, commonly regarded as one of the most aggressive Tory leaders, took no part in this chase. And—perhaps in consequence—the two ministers ultimately escaped to further promotion and honours.

Carson's restraint reflects directly upon his fundamental priorities and professional values. Rather than exploit the discomfiture of the Liberal ministers for the profit of British Conservatives and Ulster Unionists, Carson was instead prepared to defend Isaacs, Samuel, and later Geoffrey Isaacs (the brother of Rufus) from the libellous comments of their opponents and traducers. In March 1913 Carson successfully prosecuted the Paris daily *Le Matin* for a libel on Rufus Isaacs and Samuel; later in the spring of 1913, he successfully prosecuted the antisemite Cecil Chesterton for a libel committed against Geoffrey Isaacs in the journal *The Eye Witness*.[26]

When the issues were debated in the House of Commons Carson neither spoke nor voted (because of his professional involvement). This abstention represented a very considerable loss to the Conservative case, and it was, of course, bitterly resented by many Tories both in the House of Commons and on Fleet Street.[27] Among Ulster Unionists Carson's attitude caused equal confusion and disappointment: their gladiatorial champion had apparently shrunk from dispatching the Liberal government. Yet his status was such that even this apparent dereliction was accepted.

The Marconi scandal and the associated court cases demonstrate that Carson, whatever his other guises, was essentially a lawyer. He had sacrificed political gain to the traditions of the bar. He had placed profession above party; he had placed professional bonds above the demands of his adopted Ulster. He accepted the Isaacs and Samuel brief because, as he said, he was like a taxi-driver, available for hire to all.[28] He was also bound to Rufus Isaacs by the ties of a genial and mutually profitable rivalry.

It was the courtroom, and not the Conservative front bench, or Ulster, or ministerial chambers, which defined Carson's purpose. He was a clever advocate rather than a profound technical lawyer; he was a clever debater rather than an adroit administrator. He was a creature of opposition. He knew his strengths, and resisted the temptation to wade into political or

professional territory beyond his intellectual depth. He declined
the Presidency of the English Divorce Court in 1905; he declined
the Lord Chancellorship of England at least once, in 1916, and
possibly on a second occasion, in 1918.[29] When, in May 1921, he
accepted judicial office it was in the Court of Appeal, where he
could shelter behind the opinions of his fellow law lords. There
were persuasive political reasons for all these career decisions, but
self-doubt, or self-knowledge, was a significant influence. His
women friends tended to recognise this truth more readily than
men: 'I wish Sir Edward had more ambition and more self-confi-
dence,' Mrs Spender declared in 1918.[30] Lady Londonderry
expressed the same frustration in a blunt but suggestive analogy:
'he is like a Derby favourite, who, when you have him saddled and
bridled, and ready to lead out of the paddock, won't run'.[31]

The bar gave Carson a public reputation long before his
association with Ulster Unionism; the bar gave Carson a professional network which often overrode narrow partisanship.
Although he presented himself as a stern Unionist, he had in
truth many friends on the Liberal benches, and some even within
the Irish Parliamentary Party: he knew John Redmond for thirty-
five years, and never in that long span exchanged 'one single
personal bitter word'; as we have seen, he was a lifelong friend of
Rufus Isaacs and, regardless of the political risk, defended him in
court.[32] Carson represented a new generation of ambitious
lawyers who increasingly dominated the Edwardian House of
Commons and whose professional ties helped to keep partisanship in check. The political convictions of these men brought the
United Kingdom to the brink of civil war in 1914; but their profession ultimately served to keep them in parliament, and to
maintain the British constitution.

The bar provided Carson with a political style. He threatened
and cajoled. Between 1912 and 1914, at the time of the Ulster
crisis, he browbeat and wheedled with the Liberal government,
treating it as an unsympathetic witness in a courtroom.
Accomplished lawyers, such as the Prime Minister, H. H. Asquith,
recognised not simply a dangerous Unionist passion, but also a
brilliant courtroom performance. Asquith saw professional skill
more clearly than bitter conviction: he applauded, but was not
convinced.[33]

Between 1912 and 1914 Carson behaved in Ireland as theatrically and as outrageously as he had often done at the bar. He oversaw—not always enthusiastically—the paramilitary development of Ulster Unionism in 1913–14; he became chairman of an Ulster Provisional Government. But the sixty-year-old advocate was an improbable rebel—a prospective revolutionary who had spent his life debating legal niceties. This was not a radical pedigree which Liberals, reading the pages of Conrad's *The Secret Agent* or *Under Western Eyes*, would have recognised.[34] Carson was an unlikely anarchist: his chief weakness was that his opponents in 1914 grasped this fact, and relied upon it.

3

THE LAND

Edward Carson's family roots were in the professional and middle classes of Dublin. His grandfather had been a prosperous general merchant, transacting his business at Cork Hill, near Dublin Castle; his father was a successful architect, with offices in South Frederick Street, and with a home originally in Rathgar but later in fashionable Harcourt Street. Edward maintained this tradition of relentless social advance, shifting on the basis of his legal triumphs, from modest lodgings in South Herbert Street, first to an elegant town house in Merrion Square, and finally to London, and to a Belgravia mansion.[1] The family might serve, therefore, as a case study of middle-class Protestant social mobility in nineteenth-century Dublin, with a domestic progress from shabbily genteel lodgings through suburban villas to the most fashionable squares at the very heart of the city. Edward Carson's own career might serve as a case study of middle-class advance in late nineteenth-century parliamentary and ministerial politics. If Carson was the complete lawyer, then he was also the consummate bourgeois.

Early in his life Carson displayed the diluted radicalism which characterised so many ambitious late Victorian professional men. This radicalism was all the more easily assumed, because the Carson family—unlike many Dublin Protestants—had no deeply laid Tory traditions, viewing themselves instead as Liberal-Conservatives.[2] As we have seen, Carson casually defied what he saw as unreasonable authority at Trinity College. Indeed, Carson the mature politician and Carson the undergraduate were scarcely recognisable as the same man: at Trinity the later opponent of the suffragettes defended women's rights. At Trinity the upholder of the Church of Ireland defended its disestablishment; the bitter critic of the Irish revolutionaries gave his blessing to the French revolutionaries of 1789; the proponent of vigorous law enforcement urged the abolition of capital punishment.[3]

Carson was an enthusiastic advocate of the tenant interest during the Land War, and in the aftermath of Gladstone's Land Act of 1881. By 1885–6 he feared that the farmers were gaining an unconscionable ascendancy, and that the Parnellites were exploiting a narrow class greed, but he still cast his anxiety in populist terms: 'the [Parnellite] cry was only to catch the votes of the farmers, and to starve the workingmen of the city . . . [but] if they went on legislating for one class they would come to desolation'.[4] Parnellism had become disruptive and socially divisive, where Unionism stood for gradualist reform and social tranquillity. Carson spoke during the general election of 1885 in these terms, endorsing Liberal Unionist candidates in Dublin. As late as June 1886, during the passage of the first Home Rule Bill, he applied for membership of the National Liberal Club (a fact which was mischievously excavated and exploited in 1912 by Joseph Devlin).[5] The diehard Tory of later years ran for Dublin University in 1892 in the Liberal Unionist interest, and indeed was condemned by those who saw in him the residual taint of Gladstonianism.

Carson's trek from the fringes of radicalism to the last ditch of Cecilian Toryism reflects partly on his own convictions, and partly on the aspirations and insecurities of the late Victorian professional classes. Carson was only one of many young professionals with radical leanings who found that prosperity was accompanied by the embrace of the political establishment; he was only one of numerous young working-class or middle-class politicians who were flattered and patronised by landed clans such as the Londonderrys (Ramsay MacDonald was a more surprising and conspicuous victim of the Londonderrys' style and charm). But, unlike MacDonald, Carson remained unquestionably his own man, abrasively rejecting acts of evasion or stupidity—even when committed by a marchioness.[6]

But there was also, unquestionably, a personal dimension to Carson's increasingly marked preference for Irish landlordism. His paternal family was urban and middle class; equally, his wife came from a relatively modest background (her father was an officer of the Royal Irish Constabulary who had retired to suburban Dublin). Carson's connection with the Irish gentry lay not with these people, but with his maternal family, the Lamberts of Castle Ellen, County Galway. This was an ascendancy clan

whose origins and circumstances were not dissimilar to those of
Colonel Edward Saunderson, the first Irish Unionist leader and a
close parliamentary ally to Carson in the 1890s.[7] Both the
Saundersons and Lamberts owed their Irish estates to the
Cromwellian confiscations; both families owned a substantial
acreage, and both were relatively unencumbered by debt. Though
a Dubliner, Carson had a strong sentimental attachment to the
Lamberts, and thereby to the Irish gentry as a whole. He spent his
holidays at Castle Ellen, and came to associate the estate with ease
and relaxation. His first love was his cousin, Kate Lambert, who
provided an intensely romantic association with the Galway acres.[8]

Carson's landed enthusiasms had also a professional and a
pragmatic basis. He had begun his legal career as a proponent of
the farmers' legal claims, but his success soon won the attention
of those solicitors who acted on behalf of the landlord interest. It
seems likely that, in defending the landlords' claims, in rehears-
ing their arguments, Carson grew more sympathetic to their
cause. At any rate, his view of Irish land was developing in the
1880s, with a populist emphasis giving way to a trenchant defence
of property. Parnell helped, indirectly, to accelerate this
metamorphosis because he linked Home Rule and agrarian
unrest, and thereby helped to create a profitable but artificial
polarity in Irish politics: Unionists and landlords as distinct from
Nationalists and tenant farmers. Carson, a fervent Unionist who
had sympathy with the farmers, found that, after 1885–6, he was
separated from his former allies and from the mainstream of
tenant opinion. Like other Liberal Unionists, Carson had to
choose between his Liberalism and his Unionism. Some, like
T. W. Russell, ultimately saw their Liberal Unionist faith as a
paradox, and returned like prodigals to the Liberal fold; but the
majority sacrificed their qualms of conscience on the altar of
constitutional principle.[9] And this was the expedient accepted by
Carson.

Carson's professional and political commitments in the later
1880s and 1890s drove him further into the camp of the gentry.
As a crown prosecutor after 1887 he found that he had been cast
as one of the principal opponents of the Plan of Campaign. As a
member of parliament for Dublin University, after 1892 he found
that he represented one of the leading institutional landowners in

Ireland. As his professional fame spread, so he grew more expensive to brief; practising at the English bar after 1893, he was both financially and physically beyond the reach of the litigious farmers whom he had once championed. Carson's celebrated defence of Lord Queensberry in 1895, which was described in the last chapter, was symptomatic of the increasingly close professional relationship which he was now enjoying with the landed classes. His friendship with Lord and Lady Londonderry illustrates his increasingly close personal relationship with the aristocracy.

It was in the House of Commons, however, that Carson's landed sympathies were most directly and aggressively expressed. In common with other Unionist front-benchers, he had opposed the land policy of John Morley, who served as Chief Secretary for Ireland in the Liberal government of 1892–5. Carson represented the notoriously recalcitrant Galway proprietor, Lord Clanricarde, during the hearings of Morley's Evicted Tenants Commission in 1892; and he condemned Morley's Evicted Tenants Bill of 1894, and the Irish Land Bill of 1895.[10] When the Conservatives were returned to office in July 1895, and quietly adopted elements of Morley's conciliatory policy, Carson was appalled. Between 1896 and 1900 he and Edward Saunderson led a landed junta in a parliamentary rebellion against the policies of the Tory Chief Secretary, Gerald Balfour. Carson bitterly opposed Balfour's Land Act of 1896, a measure which owed much to the preparatory work of Morley, and which was designed both to advance the cause of land purchase, and to extend the operation of Gladstone's great Land Act of 1881. Carson saw in the measure not simply the preferential treatment of one assertive and violent class, the farmers; he saw the betrayal of the landed garrison which had fought so tenaciously for the Union against the Plan of Campaign between 1886 and 1891. Above all, he saw in Balfour's bill the legislative expression of Tory hypocrisy and guile—the legislative antithesis of the professed creed of the party when in opposition. He angrily confronted his old patron Arthur Balfour over the bill. He flounced out of the House of Commons in a characteristically huffy and theatrical gesture.[11] And he embarked upon a campaign of political dissent which was only interrupted—and even then only temporarily—in May 1900 when he was ensnared by the office of Solicitor General.

The last great reform of the Tory era was the Land Act created by George Wyndham and launched in the House of Commons in 1903. The general landed reaction was much milder than for many earlier purchase measures, and this was because Wyndham's bill was consensual in its origins, and not a ministerial imposition. The bill of 1896 had been a legislative fiat, whereas that of 1903 had evolved organically and through a tortuous diplomacy between the landlords and tenants.[12] When Wyndham's bill came to the House of Commons there was therefore no wrecking campaign from the landlord benches: instead there was much solemn and constructive debate over details, and much mutual congratulation. Yet Carson, more than the other landed recusants, remained detached. Only he contrived to crack this thin crust of amity: he impatiently cut through the courtly niceties and genial hypocrisy which cushioned the progress of the bill, alternately highlighting its defects and bewailing its likely impact.[13]

Carson's quirky landed enthusiasms permit some more fundamental reflections on his political creed. That he grew more conservative with age and success is beyond question. Yet he never lost his faith in gradualist reform or his sympathy for the disadvantaged.[14] Carson defended farmers in the early 1880s, when the burden of land law was weighted against their interests; he supported the Land Act of 1881 and admired the vision of its creator, Gladstone. He supported the urban poor, when political and legislative advantage shifted towards the farmers, and when Parnellism seemed to be blind to working-class needs. He supported landlordism and Ulster Unionism when—from his perspective—each seemed to be have been discarded by British legislators. In many ways, like Edward Saunderson, Carson retained a core of Liberal, or Whiggish, convictions—even in the twilight years of his political career, when he came to personify an antique Toryism.[15]

Perhaps Carson had shifted less in his career than had the median of British and Irish politics. On both islands the political centre of gravity had moved decisively to the left in the late nineteenth century, leaving inflexible but not illiberal politicians such as Carson thoroughly beached. Carson was clearly disturbed by the radicalisation of Irish politics in the 1880s, and by the increasingly flippant attitude to law and order which accompanied (and promoted) this development. He was equally alarmed, like other Tories, by the growth of socialism in Edwardian England. He saw Irish agrarian radicalism and English socialism as interrelated threats to the parliamentary and legal order around which he had built his life. Each subverted the rights of property, and therefore the fundamental basis of society; each threatened violence in the pursuit of its conception of social justice.

Gradual, considered reform was earnestly promoted by Carson in fields such as Catholic university education (in 1897 and 1908).[16] But he was not a great, pro-active and constructive reformer. He felt that to correct injustice through positive discrimination—through, for example, weighting laws heavily in the tenant interest—was simply to swap different forms of inequality. And to throw concessions into the jaws of violent agitation, as Carson believed had been done in the 1890s, was tantamount to criminal incitement.

But to unravel the complexities of Carson's landed principles is merely to expose the central paradox of his career. Until 1910 Carson was certainly a passionate defender of the British parliamentary and judicial establishment. Until 1910 Carson was racked by the spectacle of timid government and by craven surrender to violence or to the threat of violence. Yet after 1910 Carson led a militant conspiracy to extort concession from a timid government; after 1910 Carson completely accepted what he had once defined and condemned as the strategies of Irish Nationalism. The resounding irony of Carson's career is, therefore, that he is best remembered for his belligerent defence of Ulster Unionism—in other words, for the complete repudiation of what had been hitherto the central purpose of his political endeavour.

4

ULSTER UNIONISM

Carson's constitutional convictions and his attitude towards political violence are the central issues of the most celebrated and controversial period of his career—the years between 1910 and 1921, when he was leader of the Ulster Unionists. His was, apparently, a pellucid faith—a Unionism firmly held and vigorously advanced. But if the public Carson had the zeal of a counter-reformation cleric, then the private Carson was as pragmatic and as temporising as any secular parson. The public Carson promoted a thoroughly militant Ulster Unionism, with weapons, paramilitary organisation, and plans for an independent loyalist administration. He was, even for gentle Presbyterian commentators such as Helen Waddell, an almost satanic personality, who had contrived to reintroduce the gun into Irish politics after an absence of fifty years ('the one theory on which I have almost conviction', Waddell declared, 'is that Sir Edward Carson is the most sinister figure that ever influenced Irish affairs').[1] Yet, in private, just as the details of his Unionist faith were ambiguous, so too was his attitude towards physical force. There remained much of the Dublin lawyer-parliamentarian in the generalissimo of Ulster Unionism.

Carson was, as is frequently remarked, an Irish Unionist with no personal ties and few professional connections in Ulster before 1910. He was, as we have seen, a loyal Dubliner, who spoke with—indeed cultivated—a Dublin brogue (most political and professional commentators regarded Carson's southern Irish accent as a tremendous oratorical boon: 'what an asset he has in his brogue,' Asquith remarked wistfully in 1921).[2] He was a member of the Church of Ireland and an advocate of landlordism when Ulster Unionism was increasingly suspicious of Anglican supremacy and landed authority. Carson was deified by Ulster Unionists, but this was precisely because he was an outsider, above, and not within, the northern Protestant community. James Craig, by way of contrast, was a prophet in his own land, uncharismatic because familiar, undervalued because accessible.

Carson was chosen in February 1910 as chairman of the Irish Unionist Parliamentary Party and *de facto* leader of Ulster Unionism.[3] He was introduced to his followers at a mass demonstration held at James Craig's Belfast home, Craigavon, on Saturday 23 September 1911. Like his predecessor, Walter Long, a Wiltshire squire, Carson was prominent in the House of Commons and in English politics. Like Long, Carson had grown considerably in stature after the election of 1906, when the Conservative Party was heavily defeated, and when Conservative M.P.s (let alone able, articulate and experienced M.P.s) were thin on the ground. Yet, despite his increasing British prominence, Carson retained both an Irish constituency and an abiding commitment to Irish politics. Like Long, Carson was sympathetic to southern Unionism—but Carson was neither a squire nor an ascendancy magnate: he was an urban professional at a time when the interests of this class were coming to dominate Ulster Unionism. He was an Anglican coming to command a movement strongly tinctured by Presbyterianism; but he was also an evangelical who, like Saunderson, could remain committed to his church while transcending confessional bounds.

Above all, Carson was a pragmatic Irish Unionist who, while believing in the benefits of union between Britain and all of Ireland, increasingly recognised that this creed could not be sustained indefinitely. Fighting the second Home Rule Bill in 1893, he and other Unionist M.P.s had privately considered the possibility of excluding Ulster from the measure; but, given the strength of Unionism in the House of Lords, and given the veto power of the Lords over legislation, such discussions had apparently little urgency.[4] An exclusion amendment in 1893 was superfluous, for the fate of the Home Rule Bill had been predetermined by the British constitution. By 1911–12, however, exclusion, or partition, was no longer a matter for idle speculation. For with the Liberal government's Parliament Act of 1911 the constitutional escape hatch which the Unionists had possessed—the Lords' right of absolute veto—was summarily removed. Carson, predictably, had been one of the most vigorous Conservative opponents of this measure—one of the most truculent 'ditchers'—but to no avail. After 1911 he had to choose between accepting the principle of Home Rule for all of Ireland, and the fracturing of the Union, or accepting some form of partition, and the fracturing of Unionism.

Emotionally, therefore, Carson was committed to the survival of an unimpaired Union; after 1911 he was logically attracted to some form of exclusion. There were several pressures urging him along these partitionist paths. Carson, although an Irish Unionist, was responsible to, and dependent upon, a vigorous and well-defined northern organisation. Ulster Unionism had always been distinct from its southern counterpart, but these distinctions had recently acquired a more severe, institutional, aspect. The wealth and influence of Belfast business and northern land was represented, after 1905, in the Ulster Unionist Council, a body which reflected an increasingly strong northern Protestant identity and articulated an increasingly narrow and particularist vision of Unionism.[5] In September 1911 the Council considered the formation of an Ulster Provisional Government to operate, in the event of Home Rule, within 'those districts of which we have control'.[6] This debate frightened and alienated southern Unionists and inspired the first feelings of distrust; but the idea of a Provisional Government was ecstatically endorsed both by Carson and by his northern support.

At this stage Carson's interest in Ulster exclusion was purely tactical and destructive. Partition was simply a means of dividing the Liberal cabinet, both within itself and from its allies in the Irish Parliamentary Party: in November 1911 he accepted, in a private memorandum, that 'it is quite true that N.E. Ulster is the key to the [Home Rule] situation, and that the government dare not propose separate treatment, and that Redmond could not accept it, and that it may be necessary to raise the question sometime by amendment'.[7] In June 1912, after the Liberal government had introduced its much-heralded Home Rule Bill, Carson supported a four-county exclusion scheme on these destructive grounds.[8] In December 1912 and January 1913 Carson fought for his own, more ambitious partition scheme, proposing the exclusion of the whole province of Ulster from the operation of the Home Rule Bill. Once again his purpose was chiefly, though perhaps not exclusively, tactical: he still wanted to undermine the Home Rule principle, and he still wanted to be seen to be open to negotiation. But he may have been committed at a more fundamental level to the exclusion of the entire province.[9]

As late as September 1913 Carson believed that partition might yet break Home Rule: he still harboured the hope that John Redmond and the Irish Parliamentary Party would prefer a general election to the risk of a divided Ireland. After September–October 1913, however, he grew more fatalistic, and more impatient with the southern Unionists ('I do not think they have been prepared to run any risks . . . it is very difficult to ascertain what the South and West want us to do as they only talk in generalities').[10] An important transition in Carson's principles and strategies had occurred, therefore. After the autumn of 1913 Carson abandoned the vestiges of his Irish Unionism, accepting that partition was likely to fail as an offensive weapon. Partition had become a facilitating rather than a wrecking device.

This shift in Carson's thinking may be explained in a variety of ways. There was apparently evidence that the government was prepared to negotiate. On 11 September 1913 Lord Loreburn, a Liberal and a former Lord Chancellor, published an eloquent call for a conference between the parties and for a negotiated settlement. Carson believed that this was 'written with the knowledge of the government and maybe of H[is] M[ajesty]': he was quite wrong in holding this view, for Loreburn did not in any sense represent the government.[11] But the letter did help, as Patricia Jalland has remarked, 'to create an atmosphere which allowed conversations to begin sooner than might otherwise have been the case': it certainly compelled Carson to think in more constructive terms than he had yet done.[12] He was urged in this direction by other pressures. He may have been privately concerned by the acceleration and radicalisation of the Ulster Unionist campaign— by the publication in September 1913 of the details of the Ulster Provisional Government. Carson was certainly acutely aware of the need for negotiation: writing to Bonar Law on 20 September 1913, he argued that the fall-out from the Home Rule Bill would be disastrous, and that a settlement was badly needed ('I am fully conscious of the duty there is to try and come to some terms').[13] He now felt that, while nine-county exclusion remained preferable, Ulster Unionism would settle on the basis of six counties. Anything less—given the sacrifice of southern Unionism—would be a humiliation.

Carson's minimum terms for a settlement had been defined, therefore, as early as the autumn of 1913. Loreburn's letter served as a spur to arbitration between the parties, and through the winter of 1913–14 there were numerous informal discussions between ministers and leading Unionists. These culminated in December 1913 and January 1914 when the Prime Minister, Asquith, met Carson on two occasions, and offered him the 'Suggestions', a proposal for limited Ulster autonomy under the Home Rule parliament in Dublin. Asquith was probably disingenuous, playing for time and searching for political advantage over his Unionist opponents: even Nationalists counselled that the 'Suggestions' were an insufficient basis for a settlement. And, indeed, Carson had little difficulty in rejecting the Prime Minister's initiative, falling back on the demand for six counties.[14]

Lloyd George may have been equally disingenuous, but in February–March 1914 he went further than Asquith to meet the Unionist case, and he presented Carson with a greater political challenge than the Prime Minister. Lloyd George was prepared to accept Carson's principle of exclusion, but he imposed territorial and chronological limits on the operation of the principle: exclusion would apply only to those counties which voted for it, and would last (it was eventually agreed) for no more than six years. Lloyd George's scheme was submitted to the Commons by Asquith on 9 March, and formed the basis for a period of negotiation which lasted until 20 March. Carson could not respond to this offer by a simple negative, even though he knew that the Ulster Unionist Council probably would not tolerate any further concession. He therefore concentrated on what was, for the Liberals and Nationalists, the most difficult part of the proposal— the time limit—arguing that the government was merely postponing the problem of Unionist opposition, and that any Ulster county which favoured exclusion should be permanently spared Home Rule: 'we do not want a sentence of death with a stay of execution for six years'.[15] In fact he had private qualms about the practicality of county option, and quietly doubted whether the Ulster Unionist Council would accept his counter-proposition.[16]

But he banked upon Nationalist sensitivity concerning the time limit, and upon their certain objections to any permanent exclusion. And his analysis seemed to be confirmed when Asquith, in refining the government's offer, agreed to six-county exclusion, but refused to budge on the time limit.[17]

This careful political pirouetting came to nothing because of the Curragh incident. At the end of March 1914 fifty-eight officers stationed at the Curragh military camp, in County Kildare, declared that, although they were prepared to police Ulster, they would not participate in any offensive action against the Unionists: they preferred, they said, resignation to any unprovoked attack.[18] To the government, who had been planning to use the Curragh garrison in a pre-emptive assault on the Ulster Volunteers, this was a humiliating rebuke. In truth the military consequences of the incident were much less severe than the legend of a mass mutiny might suggest, and the government retained a considerable offensive capacity: General Nevil Macready, commanding the troops in Ulster, continued to believe that his men would obey all orders.[19] But the political fall-out was certainly more significant and debilitating than any military consequence, and Macready was alarmed to discover that his ministerial superiors had panicked and had abandoned any thoughts of coercing rebel Ulster. It was believed, both in the press and in parliament, that the government had lost room for manoeuvre and credibility through the 'mutiny', and that Carson and his Ulster Volunteers had been the beneficiaries of this reverse. Carson undoubtedly felt that his bargaining position had been strengthened, and he put the case for exclusion to the House of Commons with a renewed urgency and forcefulness.[20]

The military and political positions of the government were further weakened on 24–5 April 1914, when 25,000 rifles and three million rounds of ammunition were landed by the Ulster Volunteers, principally at Larne, in County Antrim.[21] Carson's followers were now, apparently, armed; they had also demonstrated superior tactical skills, smuggling into Ireland a massive quantity of armaments in defiance of a government ban and official surveillance. Yet the reality for Carson was that the enhanced military capacity of the Volunteers acted as a constraint, because it inflated the confidence of his followers and therefore

limited his own ability to offer further concessions to Asquith and
to Redmond. After the Curragh and Larne incidents Carson
simply restated his demand for six-county exclusion. It is doubtful
whether he would have wished to go further than this on his own
account; but it is quite certain that he believed that his followers
would not accept further concession. It is also clear that after the
Curragh incident, and the revelations of a planned assault on the
Ulster Volunteers, he lost any vestigial respect for Asquith and the
government, and all confidence in their good faith: this in itself
limited his susceptibility to further compromise. He was undoubtedly worried by the heightened prospects of a civil war in Ireland,
particularly after April 1914 (this issue will be examined later in
the chapter); but he registered his alarm in pleading, emollient
language, and not in any real shift on the exclusion issue. The
only (slight) evidence of more serious second thoughts is to be
found in his tentative enthusiasm for federal government within
the United Kingdom. Even this, however, seriously alarmed some
of his supporters and stimulated defensive and apologetic editori-
als in the Belfast Unionist press: in the face of opposition and an
adamatine government, Carson backtracked.[22]

He maintained his six-county stand throughout the spring and
summer of 1914, until the outbreak of the European war at the
beginning of August. At the inter-party conference on Ireland,
held at Buckingham Palace in July 1914, he was unmoved by the
pleas of King George V and by the persuasive diplomacy of
Asquith's emissary, Lord Murray of Elibank.[23] He and Bonar Law
casually dismissed the latest feats of constitutional dexterity
performed by the Prime Minister (Asquith was now prepared to
embellish the offer of four counties, by swapping south Tyrone
and north Fermanagh in return for the cession by the Unionists,
of south Armagh, south Fermanagh and three-quarters of County
Tyrone).[24] When war was declared, on 4 August, Carson was
prepared to suspend his militancy, but not his passion for the six
counties.

Carson's constitutional priorities in these years, though
shifting, may nonetheless be defined with some precision. The
second theme central to his period as Unionist leader—his
attitude towards physical force—presents greater ambiguities, and
therefore greater interpretative problems. Until 1911 Carson was

a dedicated opponent of political violence. He had struggled relentlessly against the Plan of Campaign; he had distanced himself from the Unionist hawks of 1886 and 1893. He made his name and his fortune in courts of law, and not (as with many Anglo-Irishmen) through wielding a gun or commanding soldiers. Unlike many of his Tory and Unionist colleagues—F. E. Smith, for example—he was not enrolled in the yeomanry or in the militia.[25] What, then, turned this thoroughgoing lawyer to the paramilitary craft?

Before this problem can be directly addressed, the nature of Carson's violent enthusiasms should be charted. For most Ulster Unionists Carson was a demigod, but not a military dictator. He did not create the militancy within his movement, nor did he devise the militant rhetoric of Ulster Unionist protest. Massive, threatening public demonstrations (such as Covenant Day, 28 September 1912) were planned by James Craig; and Carson's rhetoric on such occasions, though bellicose, often did not match the expectations of hardline loyalists among the crowd.[26] The rapid development of paramilitary training and drilling in 1911–12 was encouraged by Carson's violent rhetoric, but not by any more direct intervention. In December 1912 and January 1913 this popular militancy was channelled by Craig into the Ulster Volunteer Force. The U.V.F. was not Carson's inspiration, and it built upon existing paramilitary foundations. It has been widely (and rightly) interpreted as a means of bringing loyalist militants more directly under the control of the political leaders.[27]

The central thrust of Carson's strategy is illustrated by his unflagging enthusiasm for diplomacy and discussion. Here was no Cromwell, sweeping aside parliamentary debate in the interests of a vision of righteousness. Although Carson believed that the Liberals had transgressed the bounds of constitutional decency, he exploited every available parliamentary resource. The Home Rule Bill was fought bitterly through each of its stages. Secret negotiations with Asquith were undertaken, even though these might well have proved compromising. A parliamentary conference with the Liberals and Nationalists was attended in July 1914, even though many leading Unionists advised Carson that this was a cleverly devised trap.[28] Carson cajoled and threatened; he swung from moderate overtures through to cruel irony; he staged histri-

onic departures from the House of Commons (as on 19 March
1914).[29] He deployed every theatrical and forensic weapon in his
legal armoury. But he stayed in the House of Commons.
Carson's passion for diplomacy and for a negotiated settlement had good cause. His vision of the U.V.F. as a pliant instru-
ment of the parliamentary leadership was soon shown to be
unrealistic. Carson often found that he was less belligerent and
less rash than his military advisers; he was often compelled to
moderate the more defiant inclinations of his U.V.F. and other
advisers. On 15 December 1912, against the backdrop of the
emergent Volunteer movement, Carson met thirty Ulster Unionist
representatives at the Old Town Hall, Belfast, in order to discuss a
possible compromise on the Home Rule question. The only
surviving report of this meeting comes from a police agent, Acting
Sergeant Joseph Edwards, and he was unable to learn any details
of the compromise formula beyond the fact that it originated with
Lord Londonderry. Edwards reported that Carson was in favour
of concession, but that he was 'stoutly opposed by the majority
present led by Colonels Wallace and Sharman Crawford'.[30] Later
that day, at dinner, Carson and his allies were able to veto
Wallace's proposal for a general arming of Unionists. In May 1913
Sergeant Edwards reported that Carson had 'counselled peace
and peaceful ways' to a meeting of the Ulster Unionist Council
where there was considerable pressure for greater militancy. On
this occasion both Carson and Lord Londonderry gently rejected
a call for arms importation.[31]

In the summer and autumn of 1913 Carson was confident that
a negotiated settlement might be won, but by January 1914 his
mood was becoming bleaker. In the context of his failed
diplomacy with Asquith, pressure grew on Carson to accept the
mass arming of the Volunteers. He and his militant support now
grasped that there would be no speedy concessions from the
Liberal government. Morale was flagging within the U.V.F., where
monotonous drilling and dummy rifles no longer offered satisfaction.[32] The impatient and irritated officers of the Antrim
Volunteers—perhaps the most significant regiment within the
movement—were now petitioning for the wholesale purchase of
weapons.[33] On 20 January 1914 Carson appears to have been
warned by the Antrim men that if the government acted against

the U.V.F. in its present unarmed condition, then the Volunteers would be broken: it was insinuated that the supine political masters of the U.V.F. would be to blame for its destruction. At the same time the general staff of the force was beginning to investigate the possibility of further arms purchases and had commissioned Major F. H. Crawford to prepare some provisional arrangements. Confronting both the moral pressure applied from within the U.V.F., as well as the genially truculent attitude of Asquith, Carson succumbed. On either 20 or 21 January 1914 he accepted—reluctantly—the principle of a major gun-running expedition.[34]

It was a momentous decision. It led directly to the gun-running coup at Larne in April 1914. It also marked a subtle transition in Carson's relationship with his military support. His purely parliamentary strategies had been seen to fail, and his qualms concerning militancy had been exposed as dangerous and unrealistic. Despite his popular stature, Carson had never been the wholly autocratic 'King' Carson of the Liberal imagination. But after January 1914 he became more thoroughly a prisoner of his own people; after January he became imprisoned by the logic of Unionist aggression. By April 1914, when interviewed by Sir Horace Plunkett, Carson frankly admitted his incapacity to control his own forces.[35] In May 1914 his tentative exploration of a federal solution was brutally rejected.[36] More than ever before, it seemed that the command of Ulster Unionism had been seized by the hawks within the U.V.F.

Why did Carson, often belligerent in speech and manner, fear the reality of violence? The militancy of Ulster Unionists grew from deep-seated fears and impatience; Ulster Unionist militancy was part of a wider European rejection of constitutional politics (by the suffragettes, socialists, the 'national efficiency' enthusiasts).[37] Carson accepted the inevitability of this militancy, but he sought to put it to good parliamentary use; James Craig, by contrast, was more rashly belligerent, and apparently much less interested than Carson in the political applications of loyalist aggression. Carson also recognised, however, that in most circumstances Unionist militancy would be suicidal.[38] If the U.V.F. went to war without—in British eyes—sufficient cause, then Unionism would be crushed both politically and militarily. The U.V.F. could not withstand the might of the British army, and Unionism could not survive the contempt of British public opinion. Equally—and this was a more immediate threat—if U.V.F. discipline broke down and sectarian rioting ensued, then the Liberal government could successfully reassert its moral and practical authority. Carson had very good reason to fear this contingency. He had been warned, in January 1914, that the government was postponing a settlement until 'the patience of the hooligan element in Belfast is exhausted, and they begin to riot'.[39] This report came from an informant within the household of a junior minister in Asquith's government, and was treated with the utmost seriousness. Carson's speeches in 1914 were therefore peppered by allusions to the need for public order, and there were additional, occasional printed appeals for calm.[40]

As has been argued, the relative military position of the U.V.F. was strengthened after the Curragh incident and the Larne gunrunning. There were still, perhaps fatal, flaws in the military capacity of the U.V.F. But these were theoretical and therefore insignificant compared with the real political quandary which Carson felt himself to be in after April. After April, with Ulster Unionism armed, and with Asquith still immobile, Carson's room for manoeuvre had all but disappeared. Violence remained a potentially suicidal option for Unionists, since (despite the Curragh incident) there remained the risk of military failure and international political hostility. Indeed, the penalties for incitement were now greater than ever, so in public Carson carefully softened his tone: 'nobody supposes that at my age I prefer strife to peace,' he told Winston Churchill on 29 April 1914; 'only a fool would fight if there is a hope of accommodation,' he avowed to Asquith on 5 May.[41] True to these declarations, and moved by the developing prospect of violence in Ulster, Carson re-engaged Asquith in negotiations in May, only to find—on 12 May—that the Prime Minister planned further evasion and procrastination by means of an amending bill.

The Home Rule measure itself surmounted a final parliamentary obstacle on 25 May, and needed only royal assent before being enacted. For Carson this spelt the failure of the political strategies which he had pursued since 1912. His reliance on Liberal tractability had been misjudged. Militancy, which he had seen as the handmaiden to parliamentary negotiation, now clearly assumed an independent force and challenge. Militancy, which had been designed to assist the parliamentary strategies of Unionism, now became its only tool; suicide became its only means of political expression. After the failure of the Buckingham Palace conference, only the international situation saved Ireland from civil war: only the First World War spared Carson and the Ulster Volunteers from the glorious self-immolation which was the threatened consequence of political failure.

To return to the problem posed earlier: why, then, had Carson the lawyer turned to paramilitary activity? Unionism in 1912–14 had become more localised, and belligerent, and more thoroughly politicised than before. Carson, however, remained committed to the parliamentary arena, exploiting every available constitutional opportunity for negotiation. In public he blessed the militants; but behind the closed doors of the Ulster Unionist Council chambers, and at more informal gatherings, he tried repeatedly to cool the temper of his more aggressive lieutenants. He recognised that the interests of Ulster Unionism lay primarily in the threat rather than the reality of physical force. But the threat could only be meaningful if its verisimilitude was beyond question. And this, added to Asquith's (perhaps tactical) procrastination, drove an agonised Carson relentlessly towards violence. Carson could not exploit the militancy of his supporters without incurring responsibilities to them. The growth of the U.V.F. and the failure of conventional political negotiation enhanced the status of the militants and made Carson more susceptible to their pressure. By January 1914 the U.V.F. hawks were a very considerable force within Ulster Unionism; and they were by this time sufficiently strong to overcome Carson's deeply held opposition to the mass importation of weapons. Also, with the development of Ulster Unionist resistance, so Carson's dependence upon the more belligerent James Craig increased. And this further intensified the militant pressures upon him.

Carson's commitment to a Unionist blood-sacrifice illuminates the paradoxes within both his strategy and his political creed. Carson, a highly sentimental and proud Irishman, never fully understood Irish nationalism. He certainly had no faith in the capacity of the Irish Parliamentary Party to offer justice to

Unionists, even though he continually pleaded for acts of generosity. He saw the Molly Maguires, the Ancient Order of Hibernians, lurking behind the honourable frame of Redmond; he saw the Irish Party as the harsh arbiter of ministerial conciliation. He wept because his advocacy of six-county partition implied the political sacrifice of southern Unionists to their possibly vindictive enemies: he therefore treated with contempt Redmond's bold acceptance of an alternative compromise in 1914 (based upon county option). Indeed, Carson's violent enthusiasms were fired precisely because Liberals and Nationalists had cleverly turned the Unionist weapon of exclusion against him.

Carson was passionately committed to the Union. He clung to a simple Old Testament morality, and to a conventional Victorian middle-class view of manliness—a view which accepted the occasional need for violent action. He was subject to increasingly noisy and persuasive militant pressure from within his own movement. He often attempted to moderate and direct these aggressive impulses. But, while recognising the disastrous consequences of violence, by March 1914 he had come to accept its validity.[42] This insight was not attained without difficulty. Later, by mid-July 1914, when the awful logic of the Unionist campaign was becoming clear, Carson fell into a state of depression. Bed-ridden, and exhausted by a neurotic anxiety, he passively awaited civil war.

5

CARSON AND THE WAR

The ambiguities and paradoxes of Carson's stand against the third Home Rule Bill were clearly revealed during the European war. Carson had led a paramilitary movement against the democratically constituted Liberal government; he had fought to remain under the jurisdiction of a British government by subverting the authority of that government; he had threatened rebellion in order to prove Unionist fidelity; he had demonstrated his Britishness by appealing to local (Ulster and Irish) identities. At a personal level, he had appeared to betray his own convictions in proving his loyalty to the Union. It was a dangerous, demanding and theatrical performance, which involved the apparent sacrifice of secondary principles to the overriding question of the Union; it was a performance which demanded self-mutilation in the interests of demonstrating conviction. 'He was extraordinarily clever over the Ulster business,' Lloyd George (who was well qualified to judge) said of Carson; 'his calculations were almost unerring'.[1]

Carson's profound fear of an Irish civil war, and his fundamental commitment to the survival of the British state were confirmed in August–September 1914. When, on 24 July 1914, news of the Austrian ultimatum to Serbia broke, Carson grasped at the opportunity to escape honourably, and perhaps profitably, from the impending disaster in Ulster. On 30 July he and Bonar Law met with the Prime Minister and the three men agreed, subject to consultation with the cabinet and with Redmond, that the Home Rule question should be postponed.[2] When Asquith announced, on 15 September, that the Home Rule Bill would be formally enacted, but suspended for the duration of the war, Unionists saw evidence of a breach of promise. But only one parliamentary speech of protest was made (by Bonar Law), and the only overtly hostile action taken by English and Irish Unionist M.P.s was to march behind their respective leaders out of the Commons chamber ('not really a very impressive spectacle,'

Asquith sneered, 'a lot of prosaic and for the most part middle-aged gentlemen trying to look like the early French revolutionaries in the Tennis Court').[3]

Carson did not indulge his anger in any other gesture of protest. On the contrary, he moved ever more swiftly towards breaking and redeploying the military force which had grown under his patronage, and which had been such an ambiguous political asset. In early September he and Craig met Lord Kitchener, the Secretary of State for War, promising U.V.F. support for the British military effort, and requesting—as a form of political insurance—that the Ulstermen be kept in their existing units, and that they should constitute a separate 'Ulster Division'. Kitchener refused. Carson later abandoned his conditions, however, promising 35,000 Volunteers for immediate overseas service.[4]

A deep sense of relief permeates these actions. Carson had led Ulster Unionism effectively and cleverly; but he had exploited the ambiguities of Ulster Protestant loyalty and their communal insecurities in ways which, while impressive to British observers, he ultimately found deeply unsatisfactory. He was clearly happier in creating British soldiers than in preparing to kill them. He was certainly more content to sustain the Irish tradition of British military service than to sustain and perfect the Irish tradition of rebellion.

Carson's now active sense of British patriotism took him into ever more curious relationships. In July 1914 he was threatening to defy, at gunpoint, the authority of Asquith's government; in May 1915 he agreed to serve under Asquith as the Attorney General in the first, Liberal-dominated, coalition ministry. He resigned on 19 October over what he saw as the disastrous mishandling of the campaign in Gallipoli and its knock-on effects in the Balkans: he was acutely distressed by what he saw as the British abandonment of Serbia. At a more fundamental level, he was anxious about Asquith's style of leadership, and by the whole conduct of the war.[5] On the backbenches he was perhaps truer to his earlier convictions, pursuing the Prime Minister with the zeal which characterised his fight against Home Rule. All the skills of opposition which Carson had acquired between 1905 and 1915, but particularly in leading the Ulster Unionist cause, were redeployed after his resignation. Most of the leading Conservatives held ministerial office within the coalition, so Carson was particularly well placed to lead backbench opinion, and to profit from the errors and unpopularity of the administration. He commanded the Unionist War Committee (the U.W.C.), formed in January 1916 as a ginger-group and designed to promote a more vigorous prosecution of the British military effort.[6] The U.W.C. came to number 150 M.P.s and represented a formidable parliamentary resource: Carson led it to victory over the issue of conscription in April 1916, forcing Asquith to withdraw a temporising measure in favour of a more thoroughgoing act.[7]

By late 1916 Carson had become the benchmark for patriotic endeavour. The rebel of 1914, the chairman of the Ulster Provisional Government, was now setting a standard for Britishness: just as in 1914 over Home Rule, so with the war effort in 1916, Carson's efforts clearly demonstrated his conviction that British politicians could not be trusted to defend British imperial interests. And just as in 1914 he sustained a bitter critique of a trimming government, so in 1916 he mounted a renewed challenge. But in 1916 there was no danger of illegality in this action, and there was the opportunity of saving British lives rather than shedding them. Unrestrained by doubt, and freed from necessarily ambiguous strategies, Carson was happy in his complaints, and he shone: he was at the peak of his parliamentary influence in 1916, and had, for the first and only time in his career, a chance of succeeding as Prime Minister. He was—certainly he appeared to Lloyd George to be—'a great man, he has courage, he has determination, he has judgement'.[8]

Carson's scheme of opposition came to a head on 8 November 1916 over the unlikely issue of enemy property in Nigeria.[9] The government proposed that confiscated enemy businesses should be sold at auction to the highest bidder, regardless of nationality. The Carsonite opposition disagreed, and moved that only 'natural-born British subjects' or 'wholly British' companies should be entitled to acquire these spoils of war.[10] The issue itself was of little significance compared with the problems on the Western Front in the wake of Sir Douglas Haig's criminally bloody Somme offensive; but Carson was acting with that tactical discrimination which Lloyd George recognised and so much admired. This Nigerian question was chosen with a view to uniting critics of the government, Tory protectionists, and wartime jingos in a formidable parliamentary coalition. But Carson was not directly seeking to defeat the government, since he had calculated that this was not yet possible; he instead sought to embarrass Bonar Law, who was Colonial Secretary, and who was therefore responsible for defending government policy on this question. If a majority of Tory M.P.s were rallied to the Nigerian banner, then Bonar Law's position within the government would be untenable. His resignation would precipitate the withdrawal of other Tory ministers, and the whole ill-starred coalition would, as a consequence, collapse.

The result of the division on the issue was a clear victory for the government, Asquith winning 231 votes to Carson's 117; 73 Tories supported the coalition, while there were 65 among the Carsonites.[11] Bonar Law was not, therefore, compelled to resign, but he had been shown that the coalition was unpopular, and that his own position was vulnerable. The Nigerian vote also encouraged another influential minister, who was driven to despair by the serene incompetence of the Asquith government. This was Lloyd George, who—as has been observed—had been won to Carson through the Marconi affair, and who increasingly accepted Carson's critique of the wartime administration. After Nigeria, these three men—the opposition advocate, the vulnerable and nervous Tory leader, and the frustrated and ambitious Liberal minister—formed what Lord Beaverbrook called 'the triumvirate'.[12] The triumvirs differed over certain details, but they were eventually able, after extensive negotiation, to devise a united statement of conviction. This was drafted on 25 November, and called for a 'Civilian General Staff', or War Council, which, it was proposed, should have executive authority over the direction of the war effort. It was intended that this body should consist of only four members (probably Asquith, Lloyd George, Carson and Bonar Law), and that it should meet daily. Lloyd George should be chairman, for the triumvirate agreed above all else that Asquith's expansive style of management was utterly unsuited for the efficient transaction of vital war business.[13]

Until 4 December it seemed probable that Asquith would accept, albeit reluctantly, the triumvirs' pressure for a War Council. But Asquith foresaw a Council with heavily circum-

scribed powers and with a strong, though indirect, prime ministerial influence.[14] It was on the basis of his amended formula that
an agreement was apparently struck on 3 December: Asquith had
negotiated honourable terms, protecting the authority of his
office and his own dignity, while granting Lloyd George and
Bonar Law the War Council which they so craved. Only Carson
had not been successfully squared. For Carson, Asquith's fudge
may well have evoked memories of the pre-war debate on
exclusion: the Prime Minister had skilfully manipulated the
principle of partition to his own best advantage, and without
regard for the Ulster Unionists, just as he now robbed the War
Council of its value and subtly cozened its proponents.

Carson almost certainly knew that Asquith, seeking to divide
the triumvirs, was gently insisting on his own exclusion from the
Council. Personal pique, therefore, may have helped to
determine his attitude, but there were also more weighty and
altruistic concerns. For Carson the Asquithian War Council was a
mere 'patchwork'—'a system founded on mistrust and jealousy
and dislike'; it was foredoomed to failure.[15] In the context of the
war, such a failure would produce profoundly disastrous consequences. The only alternative to Asquith's hypocritical trimming
was a compact administration headed by Lloyd George.

Carson acted upon these convictions in two ways. He urged on
Bonar Law the need to remove Asquith and the desirability of a
Lloyd George ministry.[16] More significantly, on 3 December he
spoke to the editor of *The Times*, Geoffrey Dawson, and helped
him to compose the leader for the edition of the following day,
Monday 4 December.[17] This piece described and supported Lloyd
George's scheme for reorganisation, suggesting that Asquith's
power over the British war effort would henceforth be nominal,
and that his personal qualities equipped him to act as a figure-
head but not as an energetic leader. Carson's collusion with
Dawson precipitated a chain of events which culminated in
Asquith's resignation. Bolstered by the support of his Liberal
colleagues, and angered by this apparent evidence of treachery,
the Prime Minister rejected the compromise deal of 3 December.
Asquith's biographers, J. A. Spender and Cyril Asquith, explain
this *volte-face* as a direct response to the Carson–Dawson leader in
The Times.[18] Humiliated by the Prime Minister, Lloyd George

resigned. Bonar Law was thereby compelled to defend his co-conspirator, and he and the Conservative ministers threatened to resign from the coalition on 5 December. The Tory threat persuaded Asquith to tender his own resignation—'a despairing act of recognition', in the words of Trevor Wilson, 'that the process of retreat and surrender could go no further, and that the time had come to abandon a position from which dignity and authority had already departed'.[19] Perhaps he acted on the assumption that no one would be able to take his place, and that he might return triumphant to his rightful office. This was Beaverbrook's view.[20] But on 6 December Lloyd George was invited to form a government. And by nightfall on 7 December he was able to show George V a draft proposal for his ministerial team.

It has been said of Carson that, 'more than any single person, he was responsible for Asquith's fall'.[21] Carson had certainly come to despise Asquith as a hypocrite: he was 'clever and polished, and knew how to conceal his crookedness'.[22] He had formed this opinion during the years of the Ulster crisis, when what he had regarded as agreements or acts of generosity had been ruthlessly exploited by Asquith: he remembered with particular anger Asquith's decision to place the Home Rule Bill on the statute book in August–September 1914. He disliked Asquith's corrosive, procrastinating style, feeling that this had helped to make more difficult his own position in Ulster; he also felt, perhaps with greater justification, that this style was unsuited for wartime management. Asquith's genial tolerance of interminable and circuitous cabinet meetings; his tolerance of patently inadequate administrative structures; his unflappable social activity—all were judged by Carson to be disastrously provocative in the face of carnage.

It is arguable that there was a tincture of ambition in Carson's actions. As the chief architect of Asquith's fall, he was well placed to press his claims on the chief beneficiary, Lloyd George. Yet he failed to do so: after December 1916, Beaverbrook commented, 'Carson was like a man whose task is accomplished. He made no claim for himself.'[23] It seems clear that he was offered the Lord Chancellorship, but declined on the grounds that he would be diverted from the war; he also felt that, were he to come into

conflict with his colleagues over Ireland, he could not resign with
dignity and purpose while drawing an official pension of £6,000.[24]
Lloyd George's fall-back position in constructing the ministry was
to offer Carson membership (without portfolio) of the war
cabinet. Mindful of the parlous condition of his beloved Royal
Navy, and over-generous in his estimate of Carson's executive
ability, George V persuaded Lloyd George to send the Irishman to
the Admiralty.[25] And so, on 8 December 1916, Carson took office
as First Lord of the Admiralty, the first departmental position
which he had held, and his first ministerial departure from the
comfort of the law courts.

Carson's attitude to his new office owed something to his
memories of service under Arthur Balfour in Ireland. Balfour as
Chief Secretary had given considerable freedom to competent
lieutenants and had vigorously defended their interests. Carson
shared Balfour's loyalty to his subordinates, proclaiming in March
1917 that 'so long as I am at the Admiralty the sailors will have full
scope. They will not be interfered with by me, and I will allow no
one else to interfere with them.'[26] Just as Balfour faithfully
defended subordinates, even after episodes such as the
'Mitchelstown Massacre', so Carson fought for the Admiralty
Board, and in particular for his controversial First Sea Lord,
Admiral Sir John Jellicoe. But Balfour had had a steady, sympathetic uncle, Lord Salisbury, as Prime Minister, whereas Carson
answered to the mercurial and (according to Beaverbrook)
increasingly distrustful Lloyd George.[27]

Carson's own experience of delegating work had been
extremely successful. As Solicitor General he had had the assis-
tance of brilliant 'devils' such as John Simon. During the Ulster
crisis he had left much of the management of Unionism to James
Craig, and had been free to fight and negotiate in the House of
Commons. Craig's skills as an impresario and administrator
contributed much to the popular success of Carsonism. The
partnership worked triumphantly, and Carson looked forward to
creating similar productive bonds within the Admiralty.

Carson's appointment coincided with the rapid development
of the German naval offensive. On 1 February 1917 the Germans
announced the opening of a campaign of unrestricted submarine
warfare. Carson's expansive promises that Jellicoe and the

admirals would be free to pursue their quarry were made, therefore, at a time of developing crisis for the Royal Navy; and to Lloyd George it seemed increasingly that the price of unfettered admirals was national disaster. Carson's natural lugubriousness, and his repeated references to his failing health and exhaustion, did nothing to correct the Prime Minister's scepticism. By the early summer of 1917, when shipping losses peaked, the general impression among the political and military elite was that, as Douglas Haig observed, 'the First Lord is very tired and leaves everything to a number of incompetent sailors'.[28]

Inevitably Carson and his Admiralty Board were less supine than their critics imagined. An elite anti-submarine division was formed to hunt and destroy the U-Boats; a Board of Invention and Research was created under the charismatic veteran admiral, Lord Fisher of Kilverstone. As Montgomery Hyde argues in his defence of Carson's record at the Admiralty, these boards pioneered and exploited a variety of anti-submarine techniques, including depth charges and the 'Q-Ships'.[29] A valuable form of hydrophone, the Asdic, came into production in mid-1917; depth charges were being produced in ever greater numbers.[30] Several tactical innovations, such as coastal air patrols, were pioneered. But by April 1917 'the general situation was little short of desperate': in that month 869,000 tons of Allied merchant shipping were lost, whereas the figure for January, at the beginning of Carson's tenure, had been 154,000 tons. In one week alone, in early May 1917, 237,000 tons of shipping were destroyed by German submarine action.[31]

Just as general disquiet concerning Asquith had been concentrated on the War Council question, so patriotic anxiety and political calculations concerning Carson and the Admiralty came to hinge on the convoy question. At an early stage of the submarine offensive it was grasped that merchant ships might be spared from destruction if they journeyed in groups, protected by heavily armed Royal Navy vessels. Carson was ready to test the convoy theory, but deferred to the caution of Jellicoe and the Admiralty Board.[32] Jellicoe was not opposed in principle to convoys; but he argued that, since there were insufficient ships available for guard duty, the convoys would be underprotected and therefore highly vulnerable. Carson vigorously defended this judgement, but Lloyd George and an increasingly hostile press saw merely further evidence of bureaucratic sclerosis. On 30 April the Prime Minister descended on the Admiralty, took Carson's seat at the head of the Admiralty Board, and cajoled its members into action. The American entry into the war meant more Allied warships, and this meant in turn that Jellicoe's qualms were no longer relevant. It was agreed that the convoy experiment should be developed.[33]

Lloyd George was able not merely to goad the Admiralty into further action, but also to contemplate a more comprehensive scheme of reform. He had lost faith, not in Carson's intellectual capacity, or in his moral courage, but in his ability to impress his will upon his colleagues. He had been house-trained too quickly and too thoroughly by the admirals, and—worse—he had proved a willing pupil. He had been warned of impending disaster, not only by Lloyd George, but by ambitious and impatient younger naval officers such as Sir David Beatty: 'we are living on top of a volcano', Beatty warned in April 1917, 'which will blow the Admiralty and the Navy to hell if we don't pull ourselves together'.[34] Both Beatty and Lloyd George cried out for the recruitment of new talent to the Admiralty, while even compara- tively distant observers such as Haig talked of Jellicoe as 'an old woman' and bemoaned 'the incompetent sailors' who manned the Admiralty Board.[35] There emerged—indeed, it has been suggested that Lloyd George orchestrated—a consensus for reform; simultaneously a general conviction was formed that Carson, bound to a defeatist Jellicoe and gerontocratic admirals, was unequal to this task.[36] By July 1917 Carson was more isolated and therefore more vulnerable than at any stage in the war; and Lloyd George was able to shunt him out of the Admiralty with little difficulty, freeing the office for a more energetic and brutal colleague.

Carson's record at the Admiralty, his fate notwithstanding, has been the subject of some controversy.[37] But the reality was that the Admiralty had proved a treacherous office throughout the war, taxing the skills and damaging the reputation of Carson's two predecessors, Churchill and Balfour. Lloyd George appointed Carson at one of the most difficult times of the entire war at sea (Churchill's informed opinion was that Carson had 'to face the most anxious and trying time of the naval war'): indeed, it may well have been Lloyd George's intention to divert and tax an able but potentially dangerous colleague, just as Asquith had sought to divert and tax Lloyd George himself in 1915–16.[38] In office Carson, lulled by memories of skilled lieutenants in Ulster, deferred excessively to his Admiralty Board: in office, and out, Carson—like the press baron Lord Northcliffe—held an exaggerated respect for the professional skills of the army and navy. Carson, following Jellicoe, promoted a variety of strategic and technical innovations to address the submarine problem; Carson, like Jellicoe, came to support the principle of convoy formation. But both men were dilatory about the application of this principle, fearing that they were being pushed by the Germans into a potentially disastrous strategy.

Carson's managerial weaknesses, therefore, were over-dependence and over-caution. Both these qualities may seem surprising in the apparently reckless and detached visionary of the Home Rule crisis. But, as was argued in the preceding chapter, Carson was generally a more cautious tactician in 1912–14 than his lieutenants: his personal inclination was towards a settlement on the Home Rule question, even if this should be a relatively disadvantageous settlement. However, he was frequently shunted in other directions by his lieutenants. Just as in Ulster, so in the Admiralty Building, Carson could be a charismatic but also a passive leader. In both Ulster and at the Admiralty, Carson's strengths were those of the opposition advocate, and he was bereft of managerial flair and imagination. In Ulster redress was provided for these defects by Craig; but there was no such compensation to be found among the admirals.

In July 1917 Carson was moved from the Admiralty to membership of the war cabinet. He was a minister without portfolio, a post which simultaneously recognised the value of his judgement, the political value of his presence, and his administrative limitations. Besides offering a general contribution to the formulation of policy, Carson had a number of particular responsibilities. He was, as he informed Theresa Londonderry in a touchy and defensive letter, 'liaison minister for propaganda'.[39] In August 1917 the war cabinet established an Economic Offensive Committee, whose purpose was to prepare for reconstruction and the likely resump-

tion of an economic rivalry with Germany. Carson was called upon
to act as its chairman, and he, in turn, invited F. S. Oliver to serve
as secretary.[40] Both men came to believe that there would be no
immediate German economic threat after the war, and both
therefore argued that the old divisions over protection no longer
possessed an urgency or relevance and could be relegated. Carson
resigned from the cabinet and from the Economic Offensive
Committee in January 1918; Oliver remained in post until the
dissolution of the E.O.C. in March 1918. But their co-operation
had at least one important outcome, for their work formed the
basis of the government's reconstruction platform in the Coupon
Election of November 1918.[41]

Carson was a member of a second cabinet committee on
economic policy. He was appointed in December 1917 to the key
ministerial team created to address the crisis in manpower which
emerged after the bloody and futile Battle of Cambrai. He was
therefore far from being underemployed, although it is equally
true that, as Beaverbrook observed, he remained disaffected and
discontented.[42] He was irritated by the renewed, if fitful, interest
in Home Rule among some cabinet ministers; he was much more
bitterly hurt by his hustling successor at the Admiralty, Sir Eric
Geddes. On Christmas Eve 1917 Geddes summarily dismissed
Jellicoe from his post as First Sea Lord; and in January Carson
resigned from the cabinet, ostensibly because of Ireland, but
certainly in part as a gesture of solidarity with his wounded
protégé.[43]

Ireland had remained a concern throughout the war, but it was
slipping perceptibly in Carson's priorities. Like other parliamentary politicians who professed a commitment to the Empire,
Carson's overriding concern between 1914 and 1918 was for the
British war effort; his energies and enthusiasm were chiefly
directed towards securing a British and an Allied victory. This did
not mean that he felt any less committed to Ulster Unionism: 'one
thing you may be sure of is that he won't let down his Ulstermen,'
F. S. Oliver advised his brother in January 1918.[44] Nor did Carson's
increasing obsession with the war mean that he ceased to be the
Ulster Unionists' leader or ceased to represent their cause. But if
his loyalist convictions remained intact, he was nevertheless often
diverted from Ireland; and, particularly when he held ministerial

office (as he did between May and October 1915 and between December 1916 and January 1918), it was inevitable that his contact with Ulster Unionism should slacken. It was also inevitable that, given Carson's war work, and given his fixed tendency to delegate to lieutenants, other Ulster Unionists would extend their influence to fill the vacuum. Sir John Lonsdale became chairman of the Irish Unionist Parliamentary Party in 1915, when Carson joined the cabinet; H. T. Barrie led the Ulster Unionist delegation to the Irish Convention in 1917–18; James Craig, a junior minister in Lloyd George's government after 1918, was gradually emerging as a more representative and influential and more truculent Ulster Unionist than Carson.

While it would be quite wrong to argue that the war turned Carson into a centrist, or made him suddenly more consensual and flexible, it is true that the distance between Carson and some of his Ulster Unionist following, perceptible even in 1912–14, became wider. Carson was sensitive to the accusation of betrayal, and knew the limits of his influence within Ulster Unionism. But on several occasions during the war he showed that he was willing to experiment with new constitutional theories and new institutional compounds. And he also showed that he was willing to attempt to sell unpopular ideas to his Ulster Unionist following.

The Easter Rising of 1916 revealed the chasm dividing advanced Nationalism and the plain of Ulster Unionism; it also revealed a narrow but more treacherous crevice separating Carson from some of the Ulster Unionist Council. In May 1916 Asquith's government sought to add a political counterweight to the armed suppression of the rising, and Lloyd George was commissioned to broker a deal with the Irish leaders. For a time it seemed as though an agreement had been struck on the basis of six-county exclusion and an ill-defined period of partition. But Lloyd George's diplomacy had been elusive and misleading, and Carson and Redmond had formed quite different opinions of what had been agreed. Veiled in confusion, the initiative was easily suppressed by southern Unionist sympathisers in the cabinet.[45]

Carson had been genuinely anxious to reach a settlement with Redmond. He saw, much more clearly than many of his supporters, that Home Rule was on the statute book, a legislative, if not an institutional, reality. He saw more clearly than his supporters that the

Home Rule question represented a damaging distraction at a time when British military failure on the Western Front was a possibility.[46] He felt a greater sense of responsibility to the 'loyal' Home Rulers who were supporting the war effort; and he had a more pragmatic view of partition than many of his supporters. Many, probably most, Ulster Unionists had continued to regard partition as a tactical ploy devised by their leaders to crush Home Rule; but by 1916 Carson had long ceased to have any such illusions.

In June 1916 Carson travelled to Belfast to urge on the Ulster Unionist Council the argument that Home Rule was an inescapable reality, and that the indefinite exclusion of the six counties was now the most generous concession which might be expected.[47] The reception was initially icy. Delegates did not want to see constitutional concessions in the wake of rebellion; they saw no need for Home Rule, and they were resentful and tearful at the prospect of sacrificing the Unionists of Cavan, Donegal and Monaghan and the whole of southern Unionism. Carson's masterly defence of the Lloyd George initiative won over most of the Council—but there remained a dissident minority, who attempted a rebellion against his authority.[48] He had sustained some damage, therefore. And his prestige suffered all the more when in July 1916 Unionist ministers like Walter Long and Lord Lansdowne firmly vetoed the initiative. To some, like Somerset Saunderson in Cavan, it appeared that Carson had needlessly divided his movement and had shown himself to be more trimming and less trustworthy than other senior Unionists.[49]

Carson had been bruised by the affair, but he remained open to experiment, and he remained willing to submit novel proposals to his supporters. Responding in March 1917 to British and parliamentary pressure for a settlement, Carson adapted his earlier cry of 'a clean cut' for the six counties into a more subtle and suggestive proposal.[50] In this he sought to square the circle of Irish conflict in a scheme which simultaneously recognised the Ulster Unionist commitment to exclusion with the Nationalist aspiration for a unitary state. Were Home Rule to be granted, he argued, then the six counties should be excluded. This, of course, was a reiteration of the position which he had reached at Buckingham Palace in July 1914, and with Lloyd George in May–June 1916. He went further, however. He now suggested that a national consultative assembly for Ireland should be created, uniting the Ulster Unionist M.P.s at Westminster and a delegation from the Home Rule parliament in Dublin. This assembly would meet alternatively in Belfast and Dublin, and—assuming mutual agreement—it would have the right to legislate for the whole of Ireland. Carson felt that this arrangement might well, in the mid-term, allay Ulster Unionist fears, and reconcile them to an all-Ireland Home Rule parliament. This scheme has been judged as 'a sensible and sincere attempt at a solution': it was certainly neither an idle nor an easy political thrust, for Carson agreed to undertake the politically hazardous task of pressing the scheme on his supporters.[51] In the event, he was spared this risk. Carson had argued from the premise of exclusion, and indeed from the premise of a theoretically permanent exclusion. It was this feature, and not the hazy prospects of unity, which damned Carson's scheme in the eyes of Nationalist commentators such as Joseph Devlin and T. P. O'Connor.

Carson supported Lloyd George's proposal for an Irish Convention in May 1917, and he encouraged a somewhat sceptical Ulster Unionist Council to participate.[52] Engaged by the politics of the Admiralty and, later, of the war cabinet, Carson played little part in the proceedings of the Convention. The Convention and the Irish policy of the Lloyd George coalition provided, however, a comparatively painless way of extricating himself from the cabinet. Carson was undoubtedly disturbed by the remote, but niggling, possibility that Lloyd George might seek to coerce Ulster Unionists into accepting any agreement that might be reached at the Convention. But, as has been noted, his anger lay as much with the real maltreatment of Jellicoe as with the hypothetical maltreatment of Ulster. However, he judged that it would cause less damage to the British war effort if he were to resign over Home Rule than if he were to publicise bitter disagreements over naval strategy and personnel.[53]

Carson backed the exclusionist stand of the Ulster Unionist representatives at the Convention, but—once again, as in March 1917—he was prepared to promote alternatives to the 'clean cut'. After April 1917 Carson was increasingly influenced by the apostle of federalism, F. S. Oliver: he was, for Oliver, 'my special minister' (even though the two had been bitter opponents as recently as

1910).[54] By September 1917 Carson, once the immovable Irish
Unionist, was arguing to the chairman of the Convention that a
federal constitution was the 'only' basis 'upon which a settlement
is possible'.[55] Nor was this an isolated or heedless remark. When,
in February 1918, the Ulster Unionist members of the Convention
interviewed Carson, he argued that there were only two accept-
able resolutions to the Irish difficulty: exclusion or federalism.[56]
By this last he understood a federal United Kingdom, with a
sovereign parliament at Westminster and several subsidiary parliaments for the constituent parts of this federation. Ulster might
either represent one of these building-blocks or comprise part of
an all-Ireland unit. But the suggestion seems to have won little
favour among the delegates, and Carson himself had doubts
about its practicality. He saw, however, political advantages in
backing federalism, and he was personally enthusiastic about the
principle, if not its application.

In many other respects Carson's view of Ireland between 1914
and 1918 coincided exactly with that of this supporters. He
fervently denounced the 1916 rising; he was a vigorous opponent
of Sinn Féin and quickly grasped the challenge that it posed; he
was a firm advocate, in May 1918, of the Military Service Bill—the
measure which would have extended conscription into Ireland.
But Carson had never been the complete Ulster Unionist, and in
many ways the war served to sharpen the distinctions between him
and his support. His fundamental political enthusiasms remained
Irish. But the war brought Carson other causes and motivations,
and a wider parliamentary and national constituency. By 1916 he
was at the peak of his influence, acting as a kingmaker to Lloyd
George, and as a remorseless Brutus to Asquith. He had won this
position of pre-eminence not through an Irish issue, but through
his criticisms of war policy. And his anxiety for the British war
effort dominated his thinking until the armistice in November
1918. He attained high office because he eloquently exploited
backbench qualms about the war, rather than about Ireland.
When he resigned, first as Attorney General, and later from the
cabinet, it was essentially because of issues arising from the war.

The war brought Carson not only high office, but also political
damage. His charismatic defence of Ulster Unionism and his
brilliant opposition to the first coalition created entirely

unrealistic expectations among his supporters and admirers: he had smartly identified problems and weaknesses in others, but, as First Lord of the Admiralty, he had proved to be as fallible as his victims. His removal from the Admiralty in July 1917, even though veiled by promotion to the war cabinet, unquestionably undermined Carson's political standing. Equally, his resignation in January 1918, though applauded by intimates such as F. S. Oliver, was not universally understood, and was, in consequence, damaging. Carson's diversion from Ireland did not bring any neglect of Unionism. There was no sustained opposition to his leadership in Ulster, and his reputation remained high when the war ended. Yet here again, as in ministerial office, the demigod of 1914 had shown his mortality. He was more impressed by the need for a settlement than were many of his following. In 1916, with the Lloyd George initiative, he had been badly wrong-footed by southern Unionist cabinet ministers; he had been bitterly attacked for his pains by leading Cavan and Monaghan Unionists. And in 1917–18 he was elaborating upon the principle of six-county exclusion in ways which caused suspicion and for which he had no popular mandate. After Lord Midleton had independently sought to hammer out a deal with Redmond at the Irish Convention at the end of 1917, Carson and the southern Unionists were irrevocably divided. There was certainly some equivocal evidence suggesting drift between Carson and sections of Ulster Unionism; but, equally, there was clear evidence of a chasm between Carson and many influential Unionists in the three southern provinces.[57]

By the end of the war Carson was undoubtedly a more vulnerable figure than he had been in 1914 or in 1916. Politically weakened, and diverted by the war, Carson had subtly shifted ground, even on the exclusion question. By 1918 he was a tired and elderly man who had been disillusioned and disappointed by office, and who longed for the familiarity of the law courts and the simplicity of backbench politics. By 1918 the first signs of his disengagement from Ireland were already apparent.

6

VALEDICTION

After the armistice Carson sought to return to the way of life that he had abandoned in August 1914. Even in wartime ministerial politics had held little attraction, and Carson now, in January 1919, refused the cabinet position offered by Lloyd George and Bonar Law.[1] Even before the war Carson had found it increasingly difficult to lead the fractious and independent southern Unionists, and at the general election of December 1918 he left Dublin, 'bartering his university seat' (in the snooty observation of Provost Mahaffy) 'for a very new constituency in the slums of Belfast'.[2] Liberated from ministerial service, he returned to the law courts as happy as a child released from school. Free from the constraint of satisfying difficult southern Unionists, and free from the patriotic constraints of the war, Carson returned to a trenchant and provocative defence of Ulster Unionism.

It would be quite wrong, however, to exaggerate the strength of Ulster Unionism in 1919–20, or the strength of its restored leader. The chief political asset which the Ulster Unionists now possessed was the enhanced position held by the Conservatives within the revamped coalition government. When a cabinet committee was formed in October 1919 to review the Home Rule question, it was placed under the chairmanship of a Conservative, Walter Long: indeed, as has been observed, Long was a Conservative who had been unusually active in the Unionist interest, having led the Irish Unionists (between 1906 and 1910) and having sat for an Irish constituency (South County Dublin).[3] Yet Long was not—despite his reputation in some quarters—simply a Tory redneck or a loyalist automaton; he was a fluent and calculating politician who was prone to jealousy and intrigue. He had been in government since May 1915, and had often been intimately involved with the direction of the war effort; he had lost a son, a young and decorated brigadier-general, in January 1917. Long, like other leading Conservatives, had been a passionate ally of Carson and the Ulster Unionists between 1912 and

1914; but, like other leading Conservatives, he had acquired different perspectives in the course of the war.[4] Carson was now regarded with less devotion and greater irritation than hitherto; his parliamentary magnetism had been debased by his administrative failings. Ulster Unionism was now viewed not as an exciting and vibrant and alluringly dangerous partner, as had been the case in 1914, but as a selfish and dissatisfied relation, bound to Toryism by ties of blood, but not of affection.

Carson had comparatively little influence over this cabinet committee. He was out of office, and preoccupied in the courts; moreover, he alienated much parliamentary opinion in July 1919 and again, in July 1920, through speeches which revived his virulent pre-war rhetoric.[5] His noble militancy of 1914, his dire threats of bloody sacrifice in the interests of the Union, sounded absurd to men who had been scarred in the trenches and to women who bore the burden of mourning. Carson was therefore losing ground, and it was his lieutenant, James Craig, who reaped the benefits. Craig had left office with Carson in January 1918; but, unlike his chief, Craig accepted the offer of a ministerial position in January 1919.[6] This separation marked the beginning of Craig's emergence as an independent force in Anglo-Irish politics and in the House of Commons. In an age increasingly sceptical of charismatic leadership, Craig demonstrated both humanity and administrative skill. In 1919–20 his parliamentary stock was rising, and it was he, therefore, who was the decisive Ulster Unionist influence over the report issued by Long's committee and its offspring, the Government of Ireland Bill. It was Craig, and not Carson, who effectively urged six-county exclusion upon the cabinet (Long's preference had been for nine-county exclusion); it was Craig, and not Carson, who enthusiastically commended, and facilitated, the creation of a parliament for the six-county 'Northern Ireland'.[7] Craig was in much more constant communication with Long's committee than Carson. Thus the Government of Ireland Bill, through which Home Rule parliaments were created for both Belfast and Dublin, reflected Craig's preferences much more clearly than those of his chief.

Carson endorsed the Government of Ireland Bill at a meeting of the Ulster Unionist Council held in Belfast on 10 March 1920; he offered reluctant approval during the second reading of the

E

bill in the House of Commons in late March.[8] But while both men tendered their support, there were perceptible differences between the attitudes embraced by Carson and Craig. Carson, the Irish Unionist, was more comfortable in criticism than in praise; and while he accepted that the bill was better than Asquith's Home Rule Act of 1914, he expressed his support in bitter words. Home Rule, even when clad in exclusionist garb, remained for Carson an abomination; the creation of a Belfast parliament, admittedly 'a ray of sunshine', implied the painful desertion of southern Protestants.[9] Craig confided similar qualms to Carson. But as an Ulsterman from the east of the province, he was much less bound to southern Protestantism; and lacking Carson's memories of the 1886 and 1893 Home Rule crises, he was less committed to an all-Ireland Unionism. A pragmatic Ulster Unionist, Craig embodied a northern sense of identity and a loyalty to the commercial and professional interests of Belfast: he had little of Carson's romantic and nostalgic Unionist principle.

With the final passage of the Government of Ireland Bill in December 1920, the modified demands of the Ulster Unionist leadership had been met. The act provided no satisfaction, however, to Sinn Féin or to the Volunteers of the I.R.A. who had been fighting since January 1919 for a rather grander, republican design. A truce between the forces of the British crown and the Irish Republic came into force in July 1921, and this provided a window for diplomacy and for the negotiation of a settlement to replace the Government of Ireland Act. On 6 December 1921 the Anglo-Irish Treaty was signed, embodying an offer of dominion status to the whole of Ireland, and the right of withdrawal to the new government and parliament of Northern Ireland.

The Treaty gave Carson one last, brief, political opportunity. By early 1921 he was a diminished, and in some ways an isolated, indeed vulnerable, figure. He had broken with much of southern Unionism over partition; he had broken with many of the Unionists of Cavan, Donegal and Monaghan over the particular, six-county partition scheme which he came to advocate. His leadership of the Unionists in these six counties had been effectively (though never consciously or directly) challenged by Craig's mounting authority. This shift in their relative standing was recognised in January 1921 when 'King' Carson abdicated from his Ulster throne and nominated Craig as his successor. For Carson, Ulster had been, at root, only a means to an end; and it would have been an unconscionable embarrassment if the most distinguished all-Ireland Unionist had accepted the role of Prime Minister in a Home Rule Ulster. Carson, in any case, had severe doubts about his health; and he had probably harboured private doubts since the war about his own executive capacity. Carson gave his blessing, but it was James Craig who became the first Prime Minister of Northern Ireland in June 1921. In the previous month, on 21 May, Carson had accepted judicial office as a Lord of Appeal, thereby signalling that his great achievements in the House of Commons and at the bar could no longer be sustained. He saw his elevation as 'providential' and was grateful; but he also felt that he was 'leaving everything in public life I cared about', and he possibly sensed that he was about to be gagged by judicial dignity.[10]

If indeed Lloyd George had sought to silence Carson through promotion, then he had miscalculated. The ratification debates on the Anglo-Irish Treaty in December 1921 gave Carson the kind of opportunity which he had been able in the past to exploit. Carson was always at his best as an opposition advocate, and he was especially effective in assaulting what he saw as hypocritical or unjust or treacherous authority. He saw these qualities as the hallmarks of Lloyd George's Irish policy, and in a brilliantly vulgar speech on 14 December 1921 he said as much.[11] Carson cleverly traduced the Unionist signatories of the Treaty, cultivating a passion which recalled his assault on the third Home Rule Bill and upon the Asquith coalition. The speech was almost certainly an attempt to recapture his days of glory of 1916—an attempt not merely to discredit a policy, but also to prosecute its authors.[12] There was also a more profound dimension to Carson's assault: 'I was only a puppet,' Carson declaimed, 'and so was Ulster, and so was Ireland, in the political game that was to get the Conservative Party into power'. The over-brimming bitterness and the anguish conveyed by these words surely justify Nicholas Mansergh's observation that here was 'the authentic cry of Irish (as distinct from Ulster) Unionism at the last, with only oblivion before it'.[13]

Carson's speech did little immediate harm to the Treaty, which was carried in the House of Lords by an overwhelming majority: in fact his position was endorsed by only forty-seven peers. But in highlighting the grubby pragmatism of the Prime Minister and his supporters, and the treacherousness of their assurances, Carson undoubtedly contributed to the gradual development of popular Tory resentments. The speech was important, not only because it marked the beginning of the end of the Lloyd George coalition, but also because it signalled what would emerge as Carson's preoccupations as a member of the Lords. 'Ulster will always be my first love, and my greatest memory,' he had confided to James Craig in 1921; but Ulster was always external, 'a first love' rather than a blood relative, and it was to the interests of his own people—the beleaguered loyalists of the south and west—that he turned as a law lord between 1921 and 1929. He spoke angrily in their defence during the debate on the Free State Constitution Bill in November 1922. In June 1923 he savagely criticised the niggardly Wood–Renton Commission, which adjudicated compensation claims. As a member of the Judicial Committee of the Privy Council he fought for the rights of those ex-loyalists who, under the terms of the Anglo-Irish Treaty, brought cases on appeal. He frequently drew attention to attacks upon individuals and upon property.[14] Ulster was indeed his 'greatest memory', but the southern landowners, civil servants, and the Church of Ireland professional classes among whom Carson had grown up and prospered were never relegated to his memory. In his last years Carson occasionally and happily visited Ulster. But he was bound by more fundamental ties to the south, and among southern loyalists he was never a tourist.

Edward Carson, Lord Carson of Duncairn, died on 22 October 1935. He had seen the heyday and decline of the Union; he lived to witness the election of Eamon de Valera and Fianna Fáil to power in the Irish Free State. He had begun his political career as a Liberal, and he died as a renegade ultra-Tory; he had set out as a politician whose inspiration was exclusively Irish, and had matured as a leading arbiter of British government.

He has been described as an Irish Whig.[15] This is true, but it is not a completely satisfactory categorisation. He was connected by blood and by sentiment to the Irish gentry, and he retained to the end a faith in its powers. He believed in securing the best possible government for all the Irish people, but he defined this goal in socially exclusivist and Unionist terms: like ardent republicans, he did not always believe that the Irish people knew what was in their own best interests. He believed in generous laws and in the maximisation of individual liberty; but he was convinced that his Nationalist opponents acted to defame the law and to subvert civil liberty. He believed passionately in the rule of law; but in 1912 he was convinced that the injustices perpetrated by government demanded an exceptional, indeed a revolutionary, response—a response worthy of 1688. In this judgement he was closer to his Nationalist opponents than any of them cared to acknowledge. He was, according to his own lights, an Irish patriot, who sincerely felt that the Union best served the interests of his country and of his people: in J. C. Beckett's paradox, 'Carson was a patriot, without being a nationalist'.[16] His people were always the Irish as a whole, and never Protestants or Ulster Protestants exclusively.

He was an Irish Unionist. He adopted partition in 1912, late in his life, and originally as a political stratagem rather than as an article of faith. He favoured the exclusion of the entire province of Ulster from Home Rule because he wanted to retain as much of Ireland as possible under the Union. He saw such a division as facilitating good government throughout Ireland: the province of Ulster, with only a very slight Protestant majority, could never sustain any denominational ascendancy, while the government of the south would be tempered and restrained by the prospect of Irish unity. He came to support six-county exclusion because this seemed to be the best deal which he could broker for his Ulster Unionist following.

He was a much more pragmatic politician than is commonly grasped. He articulated the belligerence of Ulster Unionists in 1912–14, but he did little to inspire this militancy. In reality he seems to have consistently counselled moderation on the most extreme elements of his support. He also seems to have been a reluctant convert to the gun-running. He exploited, but undoubtedly feared, the prospect of civil war: the greater the likelihood of violence, the more earnestly he pursued negotiation and cultivated a softer rhetoric. Carson originally saw militancy as a means of conditioning parliamentary debate, as a means of extorting concessions from a British government. It is probably true to say that he originally regarded militancy as a bluff; it is equally true that the more frequently this bluff was called—the more Asquith drew out the negotiations—the closer Ireland came to violence. In the end—by July 1914—bluff became conviction, and Carson reluctantly accepted the likelihood of civil war. But this was a late and an unwilling concession, for Carson had always grasped that violence probably meant defeat and destruction for Ulster Unionism. Indeed, Carson clearly foresaw the possibility that he and the Ulster Provisional Government would part company on the issue of violence and illegality.[17]

Carson's success as a popular leader of Ulster Unionism stemmed, ironically, from the skills which he acquired in the law courts. He was a formidable orator, and an incisive critic. His intellect was essentially destructive: he could identify weaknesses and inconsistencies and hypocrisy in opponents with a dazzling clarity. He was, apparently, fearless; indeed, he combined legal gravity with an attractive streak of impetuosity. As a lawyer he made effective use of younger 'devils'; as Ulster Unionist leader he leaned heavily upon James Craig and other lieutenants. He incorporated a populist touch in both his legal and his loyalist activity: like his mentor, Lord Milner, he had an unbounded and paternalist admiration for the patriotic working man.[18]

But he was neither a profound lawyer, nor an innovative political strategist. In the courts he relied heavily on his eloquence and on his forensic skills, rather than on any more subtle grasp of legal principles: he was thus a great barrister, but he made an unremarkable law lord. As a political leader he relied more heavily upon impassioned oratory than upon clever management or strategic novelty. Carson was therefore the greatest opposition advocate of his day, but he made a barely competent minister of the crown. He was the vital inspiration behind Ulster Unionism in 1912–14, but he was not the architect of resistance: it was James Craig who, through superlative managerial skills, promoted Carson to regal and ultimately divine status among northern loyalists. Through stage-management and mass propaganda, Craig cultivated the romance of Carson, and bequeathed a mythology to later generations of northern Protestants.[19]

The skills which made Carson a brilliant opposition leader weakened him in office. He did well as Solicitor General and as Attorney General: Walter Runciman thought him 'a very adroit and resourceful' member of the Asquith coalition cabinet; Lloyd George agreed.[20] But the oratory and diplomacy which helped Carson to oust Asquith in December 1916 proved to be weak weapons in the fight against the German submarine offensive. Criticism of Carson as First Lord of the Admiralty has owed as much to Lloyd George's skewed perspectives and egotism as to the actual record; but Carson certainly made errors of judgement, and he certainly acquired a reputation as an ailing, exhausted and ineffective minister. In part this was because he relied too heavily upon overcautious and tired subordinates such as Jellicoe. When Carson was shifted to the war cabinet he was under much less pressure, and he had rather fresher and more resourceful advisers (such as F. S. Oliver): accordingly he performed rather better there than he had done at the Admiralty.

But Carson's perceived failure as First Lord was also, in part, a failure of image and of personality. As Ulster Unionist leader, Carson's illness and depression had mattered little: they had been, in fact, an asset—for Carson was widely believed to be a man who had sacrificed his health and well-being to the loyalist interest. On balance, his melancholic and fatalistic outlook, his periods of mental and physical anguish, added to his popular charisma. Such qualities were less admired at the Admiralty, where Carson's habitual complaints about his health and periodic lapses in self-esteem created panic. At least once during the war he had a serious relapse, and was rumoured to have had a stroke. Such gossip, combined with Carson's natural lugubriousness, did little to bolster the confidence of those who feared for the British war effort. Carson's successor as First Lord came like a confident and breezy General Montgomery, displacing a weary and despondent Auchinleck.

Carson's achievement was therefore negative, but real. His great contribution to the war effort and to the British Empire was certainly negative and indirect: he was an ineffective minister, but he had helped to oust Asquith, who was, or—equally important— was thought to be, incapable of leading the British to victory. Carson's contribution to Irish Unionism was equally negative: he failed to sustain his vision of the Union, and he felt compelled to settle for a compromise which satisfied his northern supporters but which provided little comfort to himself. He was often doubtful about Unionist militancy, but his association with the U.V.F. meant that he was popularly identified in Ireland as an armed subverter of the British constitution. In this way he won grudging respect among revolutionary nationalists and indirectly and unconsciously enflamed the physical-force tradition. Carson simultaneously inspired Unionist and republican belligerence: he contributed decisively, therefore, to the creation both of Northern Ireland and the Irish Free State. His tragedy was that he wanted neither of these territories. The independent Ireland of de Valera was a foreign country for this sentimental Dubliner; and Northern Ireland provided a tomb, but never a home.

NOTES

Introduction

[1] Compare Rattigan's portrait of Sir Robert Morton, K.C., with St John Ervine's description of Carson in *Craigavon: Ulsterman* (London, 1949), p. 182.

[2] J. J. Lee, *Ireland, 1912–85: Politics and Society* (Cambridge, 1989), p. 6 ('His was essentially a Junker temperament')—though see the important critique by Graham Walker, 'Old History: Protestant Ulster in Lee's *Ireland*' in *The Irish Review* (Spring and Summer, 1992), pp 65–71. See also: F. X. Martin, '1916: Myth, Fact and Mystery', *Studia Hibernica*, vii (1967), where the U.V.F. are the 'first Fascist army'; A. P. Ryan, *Mutiny at the Curragh* (London, 1956), dustwrapper blurb, where Carson's speeches are 'reminiscent of Hitler rallies'; Andrew Gailey, 'Ulster Unionism, British Conservatism and the Reign of King Carson', unpublished paper: Carson acts in ways which 'were the precursors of techniques honed by the fascists in the 1920s and 1930s'. Bulmer Hobson took a different line: 'in plain terms the Carsonite movement in Ireland was Fenianism without the noble political ideals of the latter': F. X. Martin (ed.), *The Irish Volunteers: Recollections and Documents* (Dublin, 1963), p. 4. See also Michael Laffan, *The Partition of Ireland* (Dundalk, 1983), pp 23–4.

[3] Edward Marjoribanks and Ian Colvin, *The Life of Lord Carson* (3 vols, London, 1932–6); H. Montgomery Hyde, *Carson: The Life of Sir Edward Carson, Lord Carson of Duncairn* (London, 1953); A. T. Q. Stewart, *Edward Carson* (Dublin, 1981); J. V. Bates, *Sir Edward Carson* (London, 1921).

1

[1] R. F. Foster, *Lord Randolph Churchill: A Political Life* (Oxford, 1981), p. 1.

[2] Hyde, *Carson*, p. 12.

[3] Public Record Office of Northern Ireland (hereafter PRONI), Edward Carson Papers, D1507/E/1: material relating to the Marjoribanks and Colvin biography, 1930–35. Sympathetic friends also supplied much material to Montgomery Hyde: PRONI, H. Montgomery Hyde Papers, D3084/H/2, 3.

[4] Hyde, *Carson*, pp 64, 124–5. The papers of Theresa Londonderry are in PRONI (D2846). There is a smaller collection in the Durham Record Office.

[5] Colvin, *Carson*, iii, 443; Montgomery Hyde Papers, D3084/C/B/2/164: Lady Londonderry's Political Notes, 22 Feb. 1919. Compare Robert Blake (ed.), *The Private Papers of Douglas Haig, 1914–19* (London, 1952), p. 240.

[6] Hyde, *Carson*, pp 26, 30–31.

[7] Ibid., p. 11.

[8] Ibid., pp 80–81.

[9] A. J. P. Taylor (ed.), *Lloyd George: A Diary by Frances Stevenson* (London, 1971), p. 96; Hyde, *Carson*, p. 399.

[10] Montgomery Hyde Papers, D3084/H/3: notes on a conversation with Mrs St George Robinson (sister of Lord Carson), 22 July 1950.

[11] Hyde, *Carson*, p. 277.

[12] Carson Papers, D1507/C/4: Ruby Carson Diary, 23 Feb. 1918.

[13] Colvin, *Carson*, ii, 1.

[14] Ibid., iii, 139.

[15] Ibid., p. 443.

[16] Alvin Jackson, 'Unionist Myths, 1912–85', *Past & Present*, no. 136 (Aug. 1992), pp 171–3.

2

[1] Theresa Londonderry Papers, D2846/1/1/43: Carson to Lady Londonderry, 15 Jan. 1910.

[2] Whittingehame, Arthur Balfour Papers, TD83/113/31: West Ridgeway to Balfour, 20 Dec. 1894.

[3] Georgina O'Brien (ed.), *The Reminiscences of Lord O'Brien* (London, 1916), pp 74–5, 78.

[4] L. P. Curtis, *Coercion and Conciliation: A Study in Constructive Unionism, 1880–1892* (Princeton, 1963), pp 197–200; Laurence Geary, *The Plan of Campaign, 1886–91* (Cork, 1986), p. 78; Laurence Geary, 'John Mandeville and the Irish Crimes Act of 1887', *Irish Historical Studies*, xxv, 100 (Nov. 1987), pp 358–75; Sally Warwick-Haller, *William O'Brien and the Irish Land War* (Dublin, 1990), pp 95–102.

[5] Hyde, *Carson*, p. 73.

[6] British Library, Arthur Balfour ·Papers, Add. MS 49709, f. 93: Balfour to Carson, 12 May 1890 (copy).

[7] Blanche E. C. Dugdale, *Arthur James Balfour, First Earl of Balfour* (2 vols London, 1936), i, 147.

[8] Carson suggested to a fellow Irish Unionist M.P., John Ross, that he should develop an English practice—but Ross 'found I really had not the necessary courage': John Ross, *The Years of My Pilgrimage* (London, 1924), p. 75.

[9] Hyde, *Carson*, p. 155.

[10] Gilchrist Alexander, *The Temple of the Nineties* (London, 1938), p. 130.

[11] Marjoribanks, *Carson*, i, 299.

[12] Lord Beaverbrook, *Men and Power, 1917–18* (London, 1956), p. 185. The second Earl of Birkenhead agreed: 'Carson was to me a man of fantastic personal charm, with a devastating brogue and a very straightforward and simple character': Montgomery Hyde Papers, D3084/H/2: Birkenhead to Hyde, 30 June 1950.

[13] Hyde's legal career may be traced in his unpublished autobiography: Montgomery Hyde Papers, D3084/A/7: 'Leaves of Memory: An Autobiography', pp 155–95. Marjoribanks's career may be followed in Lord Hailsham, *A Sparrow's Flight: Memories* (London, 1990), pp 45–7, 79–82.

[14] Collins's letter is reproduced in Hyde, *Carson*, opposite p. 145. For the trials see H. Montgomery Hyde (ed.), *The Trials of Oscar Wilde* (London, 1948), H. Montgomery Hyde, *Oscar Wilde*, paperback edition (London, 1982), pp 245–86; Richard Ellmann, *Oscar Wilde* (New York, 1988), pp 440–52.

[15] This is reproduced in Hyde, *Wilde*, p. vii.

[16] Hyde, *Carson*, p. 143.

[17] Ellmann, *Wilde*, p. 452.

[18] *The Trials of Oscar Wilde* was filmed in 1964 with Peter Finch playing Wilde.

[19] Hyde, *Carson*, p. 143.

[20] *Morning Post*, 25 Oct. 1935.

[21] Montgomery Hyde Papers, D3084/H/2: Birkenhead to Hyde, 30 June 1950.

[22] Hyde, *Carson*, pp 263–76.

[23] Ibid., p. 275.

[24] Terence Rattigan, 'The Winslow Boy' in *Collected Plays* (2 vols London, 1953). The play was filmed in 1946 with Robert Donat as Sir Robert Morton.

[25] Hyde, *Carson*, pp 329–34; John Grigg, *Lloyd George: From Peace to War, 1912–16* (London, 1988), pp 48–66; Denis Judd, *Lord Reading* (London, 1985), pp 90–107.

[26] Hyde, *Carson*, pp 331–2.

[27] Bodleian Library, Oxford, H. A. Gwynne Papers, MS 17: Carson to Gwynne, June 1913 (defending his role in the Marconi case). Gwynne later, in 1918, attempted to resurrect the case, but Carson counselled him against this action: G. R. Searle, *Corruption in British Politics* (Oxford, 1987), pp 329–30.

[28] Hyde, *Carson*, p. 333.

[29] Ibid., pp 205–6, 413, 438.

[30] Colvin, *Carson*, iii, 354.

[31] Ibid., p. 443.

[32] Ibid., p. 332.

[33] Michael and Eleanor Brock (eds), *H. H. Asquith: Letters to Venetia Stanley* (Oxford, 1982), p. 47; Earl of Oxford and Asquith, *Memories and Reflections, 1852–1927* (2 vols, London, 1928), i, 102.

[34] Both of Conrad's novels appeared on the eve of the third Home Rule crisis—*The Secret Agent* in 1907 and *Under Western Eyes* in 1911.

3

[1] Hyde, *Carson*, pp 5–6. For social mobility in late nineteenth-century Dublin see Mary Daly, *Dublin: The Deposed Capital, 1860–1914* (Cork, 1984), pp 117–51 (esp. pp 131–3 on the law).

[2] Hyde, *Carson*, p. 6.

[3] Ibid., p. 14. There exists a fine photograph of Carson and Bonar Law being harried by Meg Connery from the Irish Women's Franchise League: Myrtle Hill and Vivien Pollock, *Image and Experience: Photographs of Irish Women, c.1880–1920* (Belfast, 1993), 6:11.

[4] Alvin Jackson, 'The Irish Unionist Parliamentary Party, 1885–1906, (D.Phil thesis, Oxford, 1986), p. 24.

[5] Hyde, *Carson*, pp 61–2.

[6] David Marquand, *Ramsay MacDonald* (London, 1977), pp 687–92. Theresa Londonderry Papers, D2846/1/1/6: Carson to Lady Londonderry, 22 Sept. 1906 ('I am sure that the most interesting chapter in my biography will be the one headed "Visits to Mountstewart"—but how will the biographers ever really understand how delightful those visits were and why you and his Lordship have been so kind to me'). See also Montgomery Hyde Papers, D3084/H/2: Edith Londonderry to Hyde, 19 July 1950, referring to 'a real row I had with Lord Carson after that famous meeting of the Ulster Unionist Council when the three counties were divorced. I told him that whatever happened Donegal should be kept as otherwise there would be this enormous frontier. Lord Carson was very angry with me, and said I knew nothing about it.'

[7] Reginald Lucas, *Colonel Saunderson, M.P.: A Memoir* (London, 1908), pp 252–4.

[8] Hyde, *Carson*, pp 13–14, 26, 239; Marjoribanks, *Carson*, i, 375.

[9] Alvin Jackson, 'Irish Unionism and the Russellite Threat, 1894–1906', *Irish Historical Studies*, xxv, 100 (Nov. 1987), pp 376–404.

[10] Ibid., p. 389.

[11] Alvin Jackson, *The Ulster Party: Irish Unionists in the House of Commons, 1884–1911* (Oxford, 1989), pp 148–50.

[12] Andrew Gailey, *Ireland and the Death of Kindness: The Experience of Constructive Unionism, 1890–1905* (Cork, 1987), pp 189–96.

[13] Hyde, *Carson*, pp 187–8.

[14] Colvin, *Carson*, iii, 443.

[15] D. G. Boyce, 'Edward Carson' in Ciaran Brady (ed.), *Worsted in the Game: Losers in Irish History* (Dublin, 1989), p. 149.

[16] Jackson, *The Ulster Party*, pp 181, 185; Hyde, *Carson*, pp 157–8, 187.

4

[1] Dame Felicitas Corrigan, *Helen Waddell: A Biography* (London, 1986), pp 182–4. Michael Laffan, *The Partition of Ireland* (Dundalk, 1983), p. 32: 'Carson rekindled the fenian flame'.

[2] Asquith, *Memories and Reflections, 1858–1927*, ii, 194.

[3] Jackson, *The Ulster Party*, p. 299.

[4] House of Lords Record Office, Andrew Bonar Law Papers, 24/3/57: Carson, Memorandum on the Strachey Proposal, 18 Nov. 1911.

[5] Jackson, *The Ulster Party*, pp 235–40.

[6] Patrick Buckland, *Irish Unionism 2: Ulster Unionism and the Origins of Northern Ireland, 1886–1922* (Dublin, 1973), pp 52–3.

[7] Bonar Law Papers, 24/3/57: Carson memorandum, 18 Nov. 1911.

[8] Hyde, *Carson*, pp 313–14; Patricia Jalland, *The Liberals and Ireland: The Ulster Question in British Politics to 1914* (Hassocks, 1980), p. 94.

[9] Hyde, *Carson*, pp 326–7; Jalland, *The Liberals and Ireland*, p. 111.

[10] Bonar Law Papers, 30/3/23: Carson to Lansdowne (copy), 9 Oct. 1913.

[11] Ibid., 20/9/13: Carson to Bonar Law, 20 Sept. 1913.

[12] Jalland, *The Liberals and Ireland*, p. 128.

[13] Quoted ibid., p. 147.

[14] Bonar Law Papers, 34/1/11: Carson to Asquith, 10 Jan 1914. Jalland, *The Liberals and Ireland*, pp 182–7.

[15] Jalland, *The Liberals and Ireland*, p. 203.

[16] Ibid.

[17] Ibid., p. 205.

[18] Laffan, *The Partition of Ireland*, pp. 40–42. The standard works on the Curragh remain A. P. Ryan, *Mutiny at the Curragh* (London, 1956), Sir James Fergusson, *The Curragh Incident* (London, 1964), Ian Beckett (ed.), *The Army and the Curragh Incident* (London, 1986).

[19] Jalland, *The Liberals and Ireland*, p. 240; Nevil Macready, *Annals of an Active Life* (2 vols, London, n.d.), i, 180, 185.

[20] Jalland, *The Liberals and Ireland*, p. 249.

[21] See the accounts provided by A. T. Q. Stewart, *The Ulster Crisis* (London, 1967); Alvin Jackson, 'Unionist Myths, 1912–85', *Past & Present*, no. 136 (Aug. 1992), pp 164–85; Alvin Jackson, 'The Larne Gunrunners', *History Ireland*, i, no. 1 (Spring 1993), pp 35–8. See also David Hume, 'For Ulster and her Freedom': The Story of the April 1914 Gunrunning (Larne, n.d.).

[22] Plunkett Foundation, Oxford, Horace Plunkett Diary: 1/4/14: 'We discussed the alternative settlements by consent. He [Carson] seemed to like the Federal Plan.' *Belfast News Letter*, 1 May, 7 May 1914.

[23] Bonar Law Papers, 39/4/43: Bonar Law, Memorandum on the Buckingham Palace Conference, July 1914: 'Asquith was less yielding than his emissary had been'.

[24] Ibid.

[25] Lucas, *Colonel Saunderson*, p. 62n.; Earl of Birkenhead, *Frederick Edwin, Earl of Birkenhead* (2 vols, London, 1933–5), ii, 16. Smith was a lieutenant in the Oxfordshire Hussars.

[26] *Belfast News Letter*, 23 July 1913: 'I find a very curious thing, that the more uncompromising I am myself the more popular I become amongst you. I have not yet come across the man who has told me "you are going too quickly, you ought to go more slowly". In point of fact so far from urging people on, it is they who urge me on' (A voice: 'You are not going quick enough').

[27] Charles Townshend, *Political Violence in Ireland: Government and Resistance since 1848* (Oxford, 1983), pp 247–9.

[28] Bodleian Library, Oxford, Alfred Milner Papers, MS dep. 41, f. 136: Milner to Carson, 21 July 1914: 'I wish you well out of the Buckingham Palace trap. What an eel Asquith is!' A. M. Gollin, *Proconsul in Politics: A Study of Lord Milner in Opposition and in Power* (London, 1964), pp 219–20.

[29] Hyde, *Carson*, p. 351.

[30] Charles Townshend (ed.), *The British in Ireland* (Harvester microfilms), CO 904/90: Inspector General's Report for May 1913.

[31] Ibid.

[32] Jackson, 'Unionist Myths', pp 173–4.

[33] Stewart, *Ulster Crisis*, pp 116–17.

[34] Ibid., p. 200.

[35] Horace Plunkett Diary, 1 April 1914. See also entry for 16 Jan. 1914.

[36] *Belfast News Letter*, 1 May, 7 May 1914.

[37] Laffan, *Partition of Ireland*, pp 23–4.

[38] See, for example, *Belfast News Letter*, 27 July 1912: 'Do not imagine for a moment that I am foolish enough at my age to think that we cannot be put down by force'. Jackson, 'Unionist Myths', p. 181.

[39] Carson Papers, D1507/A/5/3: Constance S. Williams to Carson, 14 Jan. 1914.

[40] *Belfast News Letter*, 21 Mar. 1914.

[41] Jackson, 'Unionist Myths', p. 181.

[42] British Library, Walter Long Papers, Add. MS 62417: Carson to Long, 7 Mar. 1914: 'My own view is that we had better finish it once and for all this time, even if we are scrapped in the effort. I myself prefer to be a prisoner rather than a funk.'

5

[1] Taylor (ed.), *Stevenson Diary*, p. 96.

[2] Brock (ed.), *Asquith–Stanley Letters*, pp 135–7; Hyde, *Carson*, p. 373.

[3] Brock (ed.), *Asquith–Stanley Letters*, p. 239. Carson was certainly prepared to accept the French analogy: in May 1908 he had declared that 'it must really have been worth living at the time of the French Revolution. I dare say at that time I would have worked the guillotine!': Theresa Londonderry Papers, D2846/1/1/14: Carson to Lady Londonderry, n.d.

[4] Hyde, *Carson*, p. 380.

[5] John Turner, *British Politics and the Great War: Coalition and Conflict, 1915–18* (New Haven and London, 1992), p. 68.

[6] Ibid., p. 83.

[7] Colvin, *Carson*, iii, 186–95.

[8] Taylor (ed.), *Stevenson Diary*, p. 96.

[9] Robert Blake, *The Unknown Prime Minister: The Life and Times of Andrew Bonar Law, 1858–1923* (London, 1955), p. 297.

[10] Ibid., p. 298.

[11] Ibid., p. 299.

[12] Beaverbrook, *Men and Power*, p. 144.

[13] Blake, *Unknown Prime Minister*, pp 305–6.

[14] Grigg, *Lloyd George: From Peace to War*, p. 457; Blake, *Unknown Prime Minister*, pp 326–7.

[15] Hyde, *Carson*, p. 410.

[16] Ibid.

[17] Grigg, *Lloyd George: From Peace to War*, pp 458–9; J. E. Wrench, *Geoffrey Dawson and Our Times* (London, 1953), pp 140–41. *The History of 'The Times'*, pt 1: *1912–20*, p. 297.

[18] J. A. Spender and Cyril Asquith, *The Life of Lord Oxford and Asquith* (2 vols. London, 1932), ii, 262–4: Blake, *Unknown Prime Minister*, p. 328.

[19] Quoted in Stephen Koss, *Asquith* (London, 1976), p. 221.

[20] Ibid., pp 221–2: Koss rejects Beaverbrook's characteristically cynical gloss.

[21] Blake, *Unknown Prime Minister*, p. 297.

[22] Hyde, *Carson*, p. 407n.

[23] Quoted ibid., p. 413.

[24] Ibid.

[25] Grigg, *Lloyd George: From Peace to War*, pp 483–6. Lloyd George wanted Carson to replace Balfour on 1 December 1916: Koss, *Asquith*, p. 218.

[26] Hyde, *Carson*, p. 415; Beaverbrook, *Men and Power*, pp 150–51.

[27] Beaverbrook, *Men and Power*, pp 145, 160.

[28] Robert Blake (ed.), *The Private Papers of Douglas Haig* (London, 1952), p. 240.

[29] Hyde, *Carson*, p. 417.

[30] Stephen Roskill, *Admiral of the Fleet Earl Beatty, the Last Naval Hero: An Intimate Biography* (London, 1981), p. 218.

[31] Ibid., p. 217.

[32] Ibid., p. 219; Hyde, *Carson*, p. 418.

[33] Lloyd George's intervention did not convert the Admiralty Board to the convoy system, since an experimental convoy was already in operation: see Stephen Roskill, *Hankey, Man of Secrets* (3 vols, London, 1970), i, 380–84; Arthur Marder, *From the Dreadnought to Scapa Flow* (5 vols, Oxford, 1961–70), iv, 107–8.

[34] Roskill, *Beatty*, pp 215–16.

[35] Blake, *Haig*, p. 230.

[36] Beaverbrook, *Men and Power*, pp 154ff.

[37] Hyde, *Carson*, p. 489n.; David Lloyd George, *War Memoirs* (6 vols, London, 1933–6), ii, 1020; iii, 1170–71; Roskill, *Beatty*, p. 253; Hyde, *Carson*, p. 416; Turner, *British Politics and the Great War*, p. 102; Stephen Gwynn (ed.), *The Anvil of War: Letters between F. S. Oliver and His Brother, 1914–18* (London, 1934), p. 293.

[38] Quoted in Hyde, *Carson*, p. 489.

[39] Theresa Londonderry Papers, D2846/1/1/143: Carson to Lady Londonderry, 11 Sept. 1917.

[40] Gwynn, *Anvil of War*, p. 293.

[41] Turner, *British Politics and the Great War*, p. 315.

[42] Beaverbrook, *Men and Power*, p. 177.

[43] Ibid., p. 181. Carson's motives are still a matter of some dispute: Carson Papers, D1507/C/4: Ruby Carson Diary, January 1918, makes clear the hostility which Carson felt towards his successor, Eric Geddes, and towards Geddes's treatment of Jellicoe. Contrast Theresa Londonderry Papers, D2846/1/3/9: James Craig to Lady Londonderry, 24 Jan. 1918.

[44] Gwynn, *Anvil of War*, p. 298.

[45] John Stubbs, 'The Unionists and Ireland, 1914–18', *Historical Journal*, 33, 4 (1990), pp 879–84.

[46] Hyde, *Carson*, p. 402.

[47] Ibid., p. 403.

[48] Carson Papers, D1507/A/17/17: Somerset Saunderson to Carson, 15 June 1916. PRONI, Sir Wilfrid Spender Papers, D1295/17/2: Lady Spender Diary, 19 June 1916.

[49] Ibid.

[50] R. B. McDowell, *The Irish Convention, 1917–18* (London, 1970), p. 72.

[51] Ibid.

[52] Ibid., p. 81; Stanley Salvidge, *Salvidge of Liverpool: Behind the Political Scenes, 1890–1928* (London, 1934), pp 156–7.

[53] Beaverbrook, *Men and Power*, p. 181.

[54] Gwynn, *Anvil of Power*, p. 298.

[55] Stubbs, 'Unionists and Ireland', p. 889; D. G. Boyce and John Stubbs, 'F. S. Oliver, Lord Selborne and Federalism', *Journal of Imperial and Commonwealth History* (Oct. 1976), p. 69.

[56] McDowell, *Irish Convention*, p.162; Boyce and Stubbs, 'F. S. Oliver', p. 72.

[57] Patrick Buckland, *Irish Unionism 1: The Anglo-Irish and the New Ireland, 1885–1922* (Dublin, 1972), pp 147, 175.

6

[1] Hyde, *Carson*, p. 438n.

[2] McDowell, *Irish Convention*, p. 193.

[3] John Kendle, *Walter Long, Ireland and the Union, 1905–20* (Dublin, 1992), pp 43–52.

[4] Walter Long, *Memories* (London, n.d.), p. 247.

[5] Hyde, *Carson*, p. 444; Henry Patterson, *Class Conflict and Sectarianism: The Protestant Working Class and the Belfast Labour Movement, 1868–1920* (Belfast, 1980), pp 131–3.

[6] Ibid., p. 439. Edward Goulding, Lord Wargrave, a wealthy southern Unionist string-puller within the Conservative hierarchy, seems to have helped Craig win office: House of Lords Record Office, Wargrave Papers, A/3/2: Craig to Goulding, 10 Jan. 1919. For Craig's very different attitude in 1918 see PRONI, Lady Craigavon Diary, D1415/D/38: James Craig to Lloyd George (copy), 22 Jan. 1918: 'I have been so intimately associated with him [Carson] in Irish affairs that it is quite impossible for me to separate myself from him in this action he has now taken'.

[7] Nicholas Mansergh, *The Unresolved Question: The Anglo-Irish Settlement and its Undoing, 1912–72* (New Haven, 1991), pp 130–31; Kendle, *Walter Long*, pp 184–5, 188–9; see also Richard Murphy, 'Walter Long and the Making of the Government of Ireland Act, 1919–20', *Irish Historical Studies*, xxv, 97 (May 1986), pp 82–96.

[8] Mansergh, *Unresolved Question*, p. 137.

[9] Ibid.

[10] Hyde, *Carson*, p. 456.

[11] Sheila Lawlor, *Britain and Ireland, 1914–23* (Dublin, 1983), p. 152. Mansergh, *Unresolved Question*, pp 197–8. 'As a piece of passion it was superb, as a contribution to the hopes of Ireland disastrous,' commented Almeric Fitzroy: *Memoirs* (2 vols, London, 1925), ii, 771.

[12] Taylor (ed.), *Stevenson Diary*, pp 237–8.

[13] Mansergh, *Unresolved Question*, pp 197–8. Craig privately deplored the speech, which he thought would encourage loyalist extremists inside Northern Ireland: John Vincent (ed.), *The Crawford Papers* (Manchester, 1984), pp 14–15.

[14] Hyde, *Carson*, pp 4, 485; Colvin, *Carson*, iii, 426, 431–2.

[15] Boyce, 'Edward Carson', p. 149.

[16] J. C. Beckett, *Confrontations: Studies in Irish History* (London, 1972), p. 169.

[17] Plunkett Diary, 1 April 1914.

[18] Hyde, *Carson*, p. 315. See the critique in Lloyd George, *War Memoirs*, ii, 1018–19.

[19] Jackson, 'Unionist Myths', p. 171.

[20] Edward David, *Inside Asquith's Cabinet* (London, 1977), p. 249; Lloyd George, *War Memoirs*, ii, 1018–19.

SELECT BIBLIOGRAPHY

Edward Carson has for long mesmerised historians. Edward Marjoribanks's and Ian Colvin's *Life of Lord Carson* (3 vols, London, 1932–6) is inaccurate in some details (especially in Vol. I) but contains many references to evidence which has since been destroyed. It is written from an ultra-Tory perspective. H. Montgomery Hyde's *Carson: The Life of Sir Edward Carson, Lord Carson of Duncairn* (London, 1953), although dated in some of its interpretations, is based on a wide range of documentary materials. It has been reprinted several times (most recently in 1987), and represents an accessible and comprehensive analysis of its subject. Like the Marjoribanks and Colvin volumes, it was written as an act of piety. A. T. Q. Stewart's *Edward Carson* (Dublin, 1981) is an elegant synthesis of earlier work, with some additional reflections based on archives not available to Montgomery Hyde. There are fine essays on Carson by R. B. McDowell (in Conor Cruise O'Brien (ed.), *The Shaping of Modern Ireland* (London, 1960)); by J. C. Beckett (in his *Confrontations: Studies in Irish History* (London, 1972); and by George Boyce (in Ciaran Brady (ed.), *Worsted in the Game: Losers in Irish History* (Dublin, 1989)).

The contemporary, or ephemeral, literature on Carson merits a monograph. There are numerous highly celebratory accounts written during his lifetime and designed for popular consumption by Irish loyalists. These include: Jean V. Bates, *Sir Edward Carson* (London, 1921) and T. H. Moles, *Lord Carson of Duncairn* (Belfast, 1925). In commemoration of the fiftieth anniversary of Carson's death, which fell in 1985, Jim Allister and Peter Robinson resurrected this genre with their *Carson: Man of Action* (Belfast, 1985). Liberals and Nationalists sought to offer correctives: George Peel, *The Reign of King Carson* (London, 1914) and St John Ervine, *Sir Edward Carson and the Ulster Movement* (Dublin, 1915). The latter is a curiosity—a highly critical portrayal by a leading Irish author who would later celebrate James Craig and damn 'Éire' in *Craigavon: Ulsterman* (London, 1949).

Carson's career touches many issues central to modern Irish and British history. Some of the more helpful articles, monographs and general texts may be found cited in the notes.